'An essential guide for students new to historical geography. It demystifies the research process with a practical toolkit of hands-on exercises and timely case studies designed to build confidence, spark curiosity, and powerfully demonstrate why the past matters now.'

Jake Hodder, *University of Nottingham, UK*

'*Historical Geographies: The Basics* is a significant and unique contribution for those researching or teaching historical geography. The title in the plural form makes an insightful reference to the sub-discipline's thematic and methodological diversity over recent decades. Organised into seven chapters, the book uses understandable language, creative pedagogical resources, and rich visual aids. The authors provide relevant reflections on how historical geography can contribute to a critical understanding of 'past geographies' and envision different futures. This book will be a valuable addition for the international community of historical geographers.'

Patrícia Silveira, *Fluminense Federal University/UFF, Brazil*

HISTORICAL GEOGRAPHIES

Historical Geographies: The Basics provides readers with a thorough grounding in a sub-discipline that revisits the past through a geographical lens. It encourages the reader to pursue researching the past in a usable manner, reflecting on the role of the past in the present and how it might inform geographical thinking.

Across seven chapters, the authors guide readers through their engagement with the past, via direct encounters with archives and memories, as well as buildings, artefacts and landscapes. It poses critical reflections on how we might work with the potential gaps and fragments in revisiting the past and the ways in which we can follow traces to unearth hidden histories. In doing so, it covers both conceptual questions and practical skills in historical geography. Critical questions include; how might we apply concepts and theories to case studies from the past? How does a researcher move from an historical idea, through to working in an archive, to writing historical geographies? Similarly, and perhaps more practically, how can we find archives or historical methods that work for our project?

The book will be of particular value to undergraduate and postgraduate geographers and historians. Whether taking a historical geography module, preparing a historical geography dissertation, or reflecting on how the past might inform engagement with geographical study, this book will provide a foundational understanding of the sub-discipline for students of global history, environmental history and further afield.

Paul Griffin is an Assistant Professor in Human Geography at Northumbria University. He teaches Historical Geographies: Hidden Histories and Usable Pasts at Northumbria. His research has considered the spatial politics of labour organising and more recently the histories of community responses to unemployment. This research has utilised both archival and oral history research methods. His work can be found in journals such as *Antipode, Transactions of the Institute of British Geographers, Political Geography, Journal of Geography in Higher Education*, and *Progress in Human Geography*.

Cheryl McGeachan is a Senior Lecturer in Human Geography at the University of Glasgow. She specialises in the historical geographies of mental ill-health, including exploration of issues of crime, conflict, and incarceration. She has written extensively on doing historical geography, particularly through participatory and fragmentary perspectives. She teaches Historical Geographies of Care, Conflict and Confinement at the University of Glasgow and has supervised several historical geography PhD students. Her work can be found in journals such as *Progress in Human Geography, Annals of the Association of American Geographers, Journal of Historical Geography*, and *Area*.

THE BASICS

The Basics is a highly successful series of accessible guidebooks which provide an overview of the fundamental principles of a subject area in a jargon-free and undaunting format.

Intended for students approaching a subject for the first time, the books both introduce the essentials of a subject and provide an ideal springboard for further study. With over 50 titles spanning subjects from artificial intelligence (AI) to women's studies, *The Basics* are an ideal starting point for students seeking to understand a subject area.

Each text comes with recommendations for further study and gradually introduces the complexities and nuances within a subject.

BUSINESS START-UP
ALEXANDRINA PAUCEANU

ACTING HEIGHTENED TEXT
CATHERINE WEIDNER

LIBERTARIANISM
JESSICA FLANIGAN AND CHRISTOPHER FREIMAN

CLOSE READING (SECOND EDITION)
DAVID GREENHAM

FEMINISM
RENEE HEBERLE

MINDFULNESS
SOPHIE SANSOM, DAVID SHANNON, AND TARAVAJRA

URBAN DESIGN
TIM HEATH AND FLORIAN WIEDMANN

PUBLIC RELATIONS (SECOND EDITION)
DEBORAH SILVERMAN

EDUCATION STUDIES
CATHERINE SIMON

DRAG
MARK EDWARD AND CHRIS GREENOUGH

BIOANTHROPOLOGY
MARC KISSEL

NEW YORK CITY
KATRIN B. ANACKER

HISTORICAL GEOGRAPHIES
PAUL GRIFFIN AND CHERYL MCGEACHAN

For more information about this series, please visit: www.routledge.com/The-Basics/book-series/B

HISTORICAL GEOGRAPHIES

THE BASICS

Paul Griffin and Cheryl McGeachan

Routledge
Taylor & Francis Group

LONDON AND NEW YORK

Designed cover image: Shutterstock

First published 2026
by Routledge
4 Park Square, Milton Park, Abingdon, Oxon OX14 4RN

and by Routledge
605 Third Avenue, New York, NY 10158

Routledge is an imprint of the Taylor & Francis Group, an informa business

© 2026 Paul Griffin and Cheryl McGeachan

For Product Safety Concerns and Information please contact our EU representative GPSR@taylorandfrancis.com. Taylor & Francis Verlag GmbH, Kaufingerstraße 24, 80331 München, Germany.

Trademark notice: Product or corporate names may be trademarks or registered trademarks, and are used only for identification and explanation without intent to infringe.

British Library Cataloguing-in-Publication Data
A catalogue record for this book is available from the British Library

ISBN: 978-1-032-77524-1 (hbk)
ISBN: 978-1-032-75741-4 (pbk)
ISBN: 978-1-003-48358-8 (ebk)

DOI: 10.4324/9781003483588

Typeset in Bembo
by KnowledgeWorks Global Ltd.

CONTENTS

FIGURES

TABLES

BOXES

ACKNOWLEDGEMENTS

We would like to thank all the students who have shaped our approach to teaching historical geographies at both the University of Glasgow and Northumbria University. As evidenced in Chapter 7, your contributions to these modules have shaped how we think about the sub-discipline, and we hope this book provides a resource for students of the future.

We also wish to thank Niamh Hitchmough and the team at Routledge for supporting us through the publication process. We also thank the two reviewers who provided extremely valuable feedback and constructive direction for the book.

Finally, we would like to thank the historical geography community for its kindness and inspiration across the years, we hope this book manages to illuminate some of the vibrancy of the sub-discipline that we are so grateful to be a part of.

ACKNOWLEDGEMENTS

WHY HISTORICAL GEOGRAPHY?

INTRODUCTION

Welcome to *Historical Geographies: The Basics*! As the title suggests, our intention here is to work with you, the reader, in shaping your own approach to the sub-discipline of historical geography. The book is primarily aimed towards those new to historical geography, whether undergraduate student, postgraduate researcher or curious academic. We seek to give some introductory insights into where an encounter with the sub-field might take you, but also to offer support in shaping your own historical geography research interests. Our belief is that historical geography is one of the most vibrant, exciting and thought-provoking sub-disciplines within human geography. The range of research it encompasses is reflective of the ways in which historical geography is extremely diverse and adaptable, from studies of geographical explorers of the eighteenth century, the historical geographies of prisons and mental health, through to the spatial histories of civil rights and anticolonial movements, protests and resistances. Historical geographers have explored all of these, and much more, and it is this range of interests that has generally attracted a broad audience. Whilst these interests are wide-ranging, the exploration of the past, and multiple pasts, is what holds them together under a historical geography umbrella. This book looks to showcase these diverse interests whilst also offering some shared reflection which might cut across these elements, in order to encourage and inspire your own thinking and engagement with historical geographies.

Given this breadth, a book of this sort is no easy task. Indeed, it is perhaps most useful to begin with a clear sense of what this book is

DOI: 10.4324/9781003483588-1

not. The book is not a history textbook, nor a text structured around a particular history. It will not consider a particular time period or historical life or event. So, turn away now if you're looking for a retelling of the life of King Henry VIII or a chronological examination of the First World War. These are prominent, legitimate histories, no doubt subject to numerous academic and non-academic historical scholarship. They may draw your attention or perhaps these are the subjects that deterred you from history in an earlier life. Either way, our intention here is to open up a wider notion of historical enquiry that is particularly *geographical* and considers shared opportunities, openings and challenges in researching the past. Our aim is to provide you with a *historical geography* toolkit alongside a series of prompts and guides which might steer you towards and through your own historical interests.

Our assertion is that historical geography has much to offer for revisiting and (re-)telling the past. As two historical geographers, we have experiences both as researchers and teachers (more on us below) in discussing the merits of revisiting the past through a geographical lens. Put simply, this is what historical geography seeks to do. Related scholars seek to utilise concepts and ideas from geography and explore these in relation to the past. This conversation is equally a two way one, whereby historical materials might also inform and shape our conceptual thinking. The drawing together of geography and history is an exciting one, providing scholars with multiple possibilities for exploring past historical events, lives, objects and landscapes. This opening chapter introduces these key principles by posing the question: what is historical geography? In answering this question, the chapter continues by emphasising the usability of the past, before reflecting on some potential entry points which begin to highlight the diversity of historical geography study. The chapter concludes with an introduction to ourselves, as authors, before a brief summary of the book's structure.

We see this book as a collaborative enterprise, one in which we work together to provide new dialogues and thinking in historical geography. We use the term historical geographies in this book to highlight this collaborative nature and to showcase the multiplicity of engagements with the past we hope to convey. Throughout the book, we include a series of short exercises and prompts that will provide an additional steer in shaping your own historical geographies

BOX 1.1 Exercise – Getting started

Before going any further, and before we might impart our own reading of historical geography on the reader, we would like you to take a moment to reflect and note down your responses to the following prompts:

1. Consider a historical moment (e.g. a past life, event or process) that is of interest to you. What elements of the past excite and inspire you?
2. Try and uncover how that historical event is documented/recorded. Where did you hear about this or encounter it? Where could you find more information about this history? You might consider libraries, archives or online resources?
3. Reflect upon how the history is currently presented. Are these representative of dominant narratives or more 'hidden' histories?

(e.g. see Exercise, Box 1.1). These are designed to help consolidate your thinking from each chapter but also to offer exploratory and creative prompts for you to devise your own way of researching historical geographies.

These exercises are important for your journey through historical geography and should be returned to throughout this book. We are aware that the historical geographer has agency in determining their research subject and their approach, and our positionality remains important, generally becoming a driving force for our research practice. It can be a long day in the archive when researching something you have little interest in! Whilst we might be limited by what remains, or the pasts that are reachable, we also uncover the pasts which carry some meaning to us. As such, these prompts are designed to guide you towards your own historical geography ideas. Maybe your geographical interests from elsewhere in your studies might be applied in past historical contexts? Or perhaps there is a history you have held a long interest in and have often wondered how it might connect to geography?

Possibly your answers to these prompts will change, and some of the examples we note might ignite a new area of interest, but your own research curiosities remain relevant as we move towards researching and writing historical geographies. Our aim across the book is to give you confidence to shape your own historical geographies. We are keen for the work to be driven by your passions and interests and will provide many prompts along the way to help uncover these. Don't worry if nothing comes immediately to mind. An openness to the emergence of research interests can be a very useful way of beginning the process and we hope as you read through this book you will be inspired by other historical geographers and their work. Our intention in what follows is to provide a range of perspectives on historical geography, offering a series of critical questions that are needed for undertaking historical geography research. We will reflect on theory, method, analysis and writing. But the entry point should come from you – the researcher – and our hope is that by the end of this book you will have several options to inspire your research directions (more on this in Chapter 2).

WHAT IS HISTORICAL GEOGRAPHY?

In our exploration of historical geography, we build upon the work of those who have gone before us in shaping a sub-discipline. And this becomes even more pertinent in a discipline structured through engagements with the past. As such, some reflection on the changing tradition of historical geography is needed. What follows below is predominantly a reflection of English-speaking historical geographies, primarily drawing upon scholarship from the United Kingdom and North America. Where possible we have looked to widen this lens, but as is noted further below, we recognise the particularities and limitations, of our reading of historical geography. Broadly speaking, historical geography is concerned with the geography of the past. It has been driven by a spatial approach to the past, analysing historical events, lives and landscapes from a geographical point of view. Yet the sub-discipline has a more complicated history than this. Just as geographical thought has shifted and changed over time (see Cresswell, 2024), so too has historical geography. It has reflected disciplinary trends but also maintained some continuities in thinking about the role of the past in the present.

Several definitions of historical geography are possible, and the *Sage Handbook of Historical Geography* (2021) does an excellent job of tracing some of the nuances and trajectories in the shaping of the sub-discipline. Withers, Domosh and Heffernan (2021) acknowledge the longer history of historical geography as a shifting and changing field of research. They recognise this history by revisiting a field of study that looks quite different to how it might be taught and researched today. For example, they engage with the work of early historical geographer Edward Freeman from 1881, who suggested that the role of historical geography is 'to trace out the extent of territory which the different nations and states of Europe and the neighbouring lands have held at different times in the world's history' (Freeman 1881 in Withers, Domosh and Heffernan, 2021, p. xxvii). Freeman, they note, was very much on the historical side of historical geography, as in the nineteenth century there was little semblance of an established historical geography research culture. Here, though, the emphasis upon mapping and links to exploration reflected a similarly dominant approach as reflected elsewhere within geography at the time. The difficult and often deeply uncomfortable links between geography, exploration and colonialism are increasingly recognised. Williamson (2023) highlights, for example, the emergence of critical place name studies as revealing colonial practices of ordering and inscribing meaning to human landscapes, which already held indigenous names. The power relations of doing so are deeply problematic and reveal links between violent displacement and place naming, as well as resistance against colonial place naming.

Between Freeman and the present generation of historical geographies is a long and nuanced history of changing approaches towards historical geography (see also Clayton, 2024). The handbook noted above should be considered a crucial resource for those interested in the longer history of geographical thought (see also Cresswell, 2024) and how historical geography fits with this, as well as exploring the range of historical geography research interests (see Box 1.2). This includes an analysis of European and American traditions and relationships between historical geography and understanding mapping across time. Crucially, these engagements recognise a variety of historical geographies and challenge more simplistic notions or singular readings of what historical geography might be. This nuance is important and is returned to throughout this book. However, we are admittedly less concerned with a detailed history of the sub-discipline and are instead more interested in how the discipline as it is now might shape research in the present and future. As such, we

BOX 1.2 Some historical geography resources

Whilst this book is aimed as an introductory text, there are several other resources and places which can help in shaping your historical geography endeavours. Many of these are drawn upon in what follows. A list is provided below with some groups and texts which might help build your approach.

Journal of Historical Geography

The *Journal of Historical Geography* publishes articles on all aspects of historical geography and cognate fields in the social sciences, arts and humanities. As well as hosting original research papers and special issues of interest to a wide international and interdisciplinary readership, the journal encourages agenda-setting interventions into methodological and conceptual debates and new challenges facing researchers in the field (https://www.sciencedirect.com/journal/journal-of-historical-geography).

Sage Handbook of Historical Geography

Historical geography is an active, theoretically informed and vibrant field of study within modern geography, with strong interdisciplinary connections with the humanities and the social sciences. The *SAGE Handbook of Historical Geography* provides an international and in-depth overview of the field with chapters that examine the history, present condition and future significance of historical geography in relation to recent developments and current research.

Historical Geography section in *Geography Compass*

Geography Compass is an authoritative and accessible geography journal publishing peer-reviewed surveys with a primary focus on human geography. This section focuses upon contributions from historical geography and provides several entry points for shaping literature reviews on key sub-discipline research topics and theoretical approaches. The journal is particularly noteworthy for recent efforts to cover a wider international base of historical geography (see for example Ding, 2021) as well as what Ferretti (2019) describes as 'other geographical traditions', including those from Latin America (https://compass.onlinelibrary.wiley.com/journal/17498198).

Historical Geography Journal

Historical Geography is an annual journal that publishes scholarly articles, book reviews, conference reports and commentaries. The journal encourages an interdisciplinary and international dialogue among scholars, professionals and students interested in geographic perspectives on the past. Concerned with maintaining historical geography's ongoing intellectual contribution to social scientific and humanities-based disciplines, *Historical Geography* is especially committed to presenting the work of emerging scholars. *Historical Geography* is the official journal of the Historical Geography Specialty Group of the American Association of Geographers. Members of the group receive subscriptions as a benefit of membership (https://nebraskapress-journals.unl.edu/journal/historical-geography/).

Historical Geography Research Group

The Historical Geography Research Group aims to initiate and foster research in the field of Historical Geography; to promote discussion by means of meetings and conferences; to further co-operation between cognate disciplines and organisations; and to generate the publication of regular issues of the research series (in the form of either monographs or collections of essays) (https://hgrg.org.uk/about-us/).

Rede Brasilis Network (Brazilian Network of History of Geography)

Whilst recognising the largely anglophone reading of historical geography as presented in this book, we also wish to highlight the vibrancy of an international historical geography. The Rede Brasilis Network is one such example. The group is responsible for organising seminars and conferences in Brazil. They also publish a journal – *Terra Brasilis* (https://redebrasilis.net/).

now turn to a moment that shifted historical geography towards an approach that is more closely associated with the look and feel of historical geography research in the present.

This book takes a particular entry point and one with a relatively recent history. Rather than tracing the history of a sub-discipline, we utilise the 1970s as our entry point for reflecting on what historical geography is now and what it might be moving forward. It is this moment that moved the sub-discipline towards something familiar to that which we might recognise now. This was also a key moment within geographical thought more widely whereby the discipline began to respond to changes in the world beyond the academy (Cresswell, 2024). As such, geography has its own disciplinary history and one that historical geographers themselves have long reflected upon. At this moment in time, the discipline was marked by a shift beyond spatial science, and particular forms of mapping social phenomenon, prompting geographers to question the 'real world' value of their research and reflecting upon the ways in which their research subjects connect to the issues and challenges of the worlds beyond the university. In particular, scholars were noting the civil rights, workers' and anti-war movements, that were powerfully illuminating the challenges of the time. Geography faced questions about its future. Historical geography was no different.

In response, historical geography became increasingly diverse in its approach, replicating these wider disciplinary challenges. Historical geography research was increasingly informed by theoretical approaches and turned towards the past with a greater orientation towards the ways in which multiple pasts, presents and futures might be viewed in connected terms. This might seem a relatively simple premise but it posed a crucial questioning of *why* we research particular pasts. Questions of social justice became increasingly prominent causing several historical geographers to question the relevance of their pursuits. Change was not necessarily sudden or overnight, but disciplinary debates undoubtedly shaped the sub-discipline as we know it today.

Taking this moment as a turning point for historical geography is noteworthy because of the emergence of several key resources and reference points. For example, in 1973 the Historical Geography Research Group was established within the Royal Geographical Society (RGS). To this day it remains a key organising group for historical geography thinking. Similarly, the *Journal of Historical Geography* emerged in 1975 and is a key resource for any historical geography scholar. In the United States, the *Historical Geography Newsletter* was first published in 1979 and similar research groups emerged across the United States too. These journals and research groups look quite different half a century on but their establishment in the 1970s makes that period a significant one in establishing the related research interests. It also shaped the way in which historical geography is understood and practiced.

For example, it is now far more likely that your engagement with historical geography will be informed by theoretical perspectives, considering how and in what way the past might be revisited with conceptual tools and wider theoretical reflection (more on this in Chapter 4). Similarly, the topics of research have undoubtedly widened and moved towards subjects, processes and places that might be justified through their links to present or future issues. For example, historical geographers are now at the forefront of reflecting on the histories of slavery, the histories of political struggles and the histories of environmental change. Although still grounded in past lives and experiences, they are notable for their connections to contemporary debates and for implementing and encouraging change in the future.

HISTORICAL GEOGRAPHY AND THE HISTORICAL GEOGRAPHER

This leads us to consider how we might encounter historical geography in the present. It is a sub-discipline of great diversity and wide ranging theoretical and conceptual interest. A cursory look at the *Journal of Historical Geography* or attendance at a Historical Geography conference or seminar is likely to encounter any number of theoretical and empirical focuses. These include studies of postcolonialism, anticolonialism and decolonising processes; feminist historical geographies; deindustrialisation and memory; histories of science; rural historical geographies and historical geographies of carceral spaces to name but a few. This diversity has been recognised by historical geographers and is representative of the way in which historical geography might be defined. Historical geographer Mike Heffernan, for example, has described it in the following terms:

> Historical geography is a sub-discipline of human geography concerned with the geographies of the past and with the influence of the past in shaping the geographies of the present and the future.

(Heffernan, 2009, p. 332)

Similarly, Withers et al. highlight how:

> Historical geography is a vibrant scholarly pursuit whose essential concern, differently realised, is with the geographies of the human past. It has a complex history, indeed histories, multiple geographies and different thematic concerns, now and in the past.
> (Withers, Domosh and Heffernan, 2021, p. xxviii)

These more open definitions are useful for what follows. We are not here to set boundaries or limits on what historical geography might be. Instead, we want to encourage creativity and innovation in engaging with the past, whilst also recognising a range of skills and influences that might assist with that exploration. Given these definitions, one might ask what counts as the past? And this relatively simple question, might not have such a simple answer (a theme we will return to in Chapter 4).

The opening up of historical geography reveals research agendas that may explore potentially anything with an historical imprint. This isn't to say, though, that our research is carried out without purpose or direction. In fact, it is quite the opposite. The events of one hour previous might become historically significant, but it is perhaps more likely that they might not invite immediate study. Thus, one of the questions we pose here is what makes certain histories matter and how are they recorded for future study. The question of what is the past, becomes instead how is the past documented, recorded, retold and remembered? Similarly, who is able to shape how the past is remembered and understood, and in what ways? These questions might appear quite general or abstract but as we proceed, we hope they will become more grounded and nuanced. Indeed, we might even question how we conceptualise temporality, or our understanding of time, in order to reflect upon how particular pasts matter at particular times. Is our task simply to retell history in a chronological manner, or might more critical and creative approaches explore past historical moments in a more horizontal, relational manner?

Historical geography, then, is informed by a critical questioning of why and how we might engage with the past. What is it that draws attention to particular histories in particular moments? Similarly, why are some histories more dominant within public consciousness? These questions point towards the power relations of constructing the past. One that we will return throughout this book, as well as offering insights into how these more dominant narratives might be contested, through community and grassroot approaches to working with the past. These practices of providing access to the past, and the act of historical retrieval will be considered in greater depth in Chapter 3.

One thing that will become clear quite quickly as you engage with this text is the emphasis upon space, place and temporality. The book is situated within geography and as such the relationship between space and time will be reflected upon. Indeed, the following chapter reflects upon sparking curiosity across a range of geographical scales. The ideas of geography remain relevant when thinking about how we best understand places and their geographies. An earlier reflection from Jean Mitchell is salient in this regard:

> Historical geography is a still greater mystery; few go further than a belief that it is about 'old' maps, and perhaps concerns itself too with the tales of ancient mariners, medieval travellers and merchant adventurers. Some feel that it is an unsound attempt by geographers to explain history, and think that the historical geographer is most certainly trespassing and probably should be prosecuted. This is not so, **the historical geographer is a geographer first, last and all the time.**
>
> (Mitchell, 1954, pp. 1–2, emphasis added)

The historical geographer is then, perhaps, still a lesser-known figure. The historian holds a familiarity to a wider public and is often found on our TV screens, within popular books or as a prominent part of education systems. The historical geographer is perhaps more modest, and less visible, but as Mitchell suggests remains an important part of the geographical discipline being a geographer first and foremost. We'll unpack what this means in later chapters, but for now it is important to stress that the primary interests of human geographers (of understanding place, spatial relations, landscapes and time) are similarly those of historical geographers. The two are closer in approach than might be assumed.

THE PAST MATTERS

Historical Geography then has its own history. What it means to be a historical geographer has shifted and changed over time. In this moment, we would suggest that historical geography can be viewed as an increasingly critical and theoretically informed sub-discipline. These terms are not mentioned here to detract or deter you from further engagement. Instead, they reflect how historical geography has become less concerned with a narrow definition of what counts as historical geography and instead have geared more towards questions of how and why we explore the past. These questions undoubtedly shape the subjects to be explored, but their asking poses an epistemological question for the researcher before they tread foot in the past. They are important prompts for us to justify our studies and to provoke careful thought before embarking upon our excavations of the past.

With this in mind, historical geography work has been increasingly justified through its relationships with the present. Scholars have argued that we might consider the usability of the past, reflect on why we revisit certain histories and critically consider the role of history beyond the academy (Griffin, 2018). This section considers these questions further by examining some recent examples where

---

BOX 1.3 Exercise – Reading historical geography

Using one of the sources identified in Box 1.2 – find one article or chapter of interest.

Consider the following questions/prompts:

1. What is the subject of the article you have found? What connections with geography are established?
2. Are any methods highlighted or utilised? Does the article indicate an engagement with archives, oral histories or other forms of the past?
3. Does the article identify any theoretical influences or contributions?

These questions will inform much of what follows in the book – we will provide a series of tools and prompts to assist you in thinking about what historical geography might be.

the relevance of the past has been undeniable, and how contemporary events have steered researchers back to the archive to shine light on particular histories. In this regard, historical geography does not operate in isolation from real world events. Interest in history is often prompted and powered by societal matters, providing justification for the geographer to step into the past.

In what follows three examples are briefly introduced to question how might you justify your engagement with a past life, event, or landscape? Each example offers a slightly different insight into what the book goes on to explore. The first example considers the relationship between anti-racism and explorations of the past; we then reflect on contemporary political matters and how they are archived for the future; finally the chapter introduces some practices of colonial archiving alongside decolonial approaches which have pushed researchers to rethink how the past is constructed, represented and told.

CONFRONTING THE PAST – ANTI-RACISM AND PROTEST

On 7 June 2020 Black Lives Matter protestors pulled down a statue of a historical slave trader in Bristol, UK. The monument was of Edward Colston (1636–1721) who, as Tim Cole (2023) notes, was Deputy Governor of the Royal African Company that was the lead British agent in the slave trade until 1698. The statue had stood since 1895 in Bristol city centre and its pulling down was a symbolic moment in the history of British anti-racism. The protestors then dragged the statue to the Bristol docks and dumped the statue in the water. The scenes held global news attention and followed a long history of anti-racist resistance targeting monuments of slavery aimed, at least in part, towards the contentious presence of the past in the present. It provides a powerful example of the lingering presence of the histories of slavery within our built environments. Buildings, statues and street names serve as reminders of the past. These might be easily ignored but for some they can prove hurtful and damaging through encounters in everyday life (passing a statue on a walk to work, a drive to see friends, a morning run) through their very presence. As such, they relate closely to human geography's interests in the built environment and meaning of place (Figures 1.1 and 1.2).

Figure 1.1 Black Lives Matter placard.

Source: Shutterstock: Armani A.

The case in Bristol is a poignant one, with its meaning and repercussions still being shaped. Indeed, the court cases of the 'Colston Four', those charged as responsible for the actions, were only cleared in 2022. For our purposes here, it also shines light on a series of entry points for the historical geographer. It draws attention between contemporary events, geographical solidarities and longer lasting histories. Black Lives Matter protestors drew direct connections between the police violence towards black communities (the 2020 murder of George Floyd in particular) and their own surroundings and built environments. The protests were a moment where the history of Bristol, and the city's links to histories of slavery, trade and empire, came to the fore as a form of resistance. Yet, for many, the presence of a slave trade statue was also an everyday experience. Walking past a monument was a daily reminder of slavery, a statue commemorating somebody so integral to the most violent form of human exploitation was deeply offensive to many.

The future of the statue remains a contested one. Should it be held in a museum? If so, in what form? Should it be cleaned and returned to its former aesthetic, or should it retain the marks of a

Figure 1.2 Colston statue plinth in Bristol – a statue moved.

Source: Shutterstock: Kendal Swart.

protest to reflect its changing fate? Something as simple as whether to hold the statue horizontally or vertically might reflect on the challenges relating to how the statue is represented. For more on these questions, see the excellent article by Tim Cole (2023) that considers closely both the public perception of the changing place of the statue and the uncertainty around how best to manage its future. For our purposes here, though, the example is introduced to foreground the ever-present presence of the past in the present. So many elements of our worlds contain histories and memories which might be propelled into a wider relevance depending on events and actions. Protest movements often prompt an examining of how the past informs the present and in this instance that questioning came to the fore. Similar processes are prominent elsewhere with statues and their meaning continually shifting and changing over time. They are both a fixed memorial to the past (at least until a change occurs), but also a symbol with ever changing, and contested meaning. As historical geographers, our interest might be in tracing not only the lives of those remembered in these ways, but also the surrounding histories that link with the monument, building, object or landscape.

More specifically, in terms of Black geographies and a commitment to anti-racism, the study of slavery, racialised violence and anti-racist resistance has been a prominent feature of historical geography study. One case study is provided below through the work of Caroline Bressey which might provide a useful entry point for those interested in considering this further. In this regard, historical geographers are increasingly responding to the challenges we see beyond the academy. Working with a range of partners and institutions, historical geographers are able to shine light on challenging histories and draw attention towards stories previously untold or downplayed. Contemporary events and social justice movements are not outside of the remit of the historical geographer, instead they are often the prompts and steers towards our next research projects. Similarly, we might find our motivation from a quieter, more personal and intimate place. Perhaps a self-motivation towards revisiting a past that matters to you, a building, an object, a plaque or a statue as an object of meaningful enquiry for further study. The starting point becomes the thing, object, moment or the curious observation, and from there your research journey can begin.

BOX 1.4 Case study – Historical geography in action – Caroline Bressey

Anti-racist and Black Geographies have become increasingly influential, shaping disciplinary approaches. Historical geography is similar, and the work of Caroline Bressey is pertinent here. To accompany this chapter, we suggest that you might also read her short 2014 article in *Journal of Historical Geography*:

'Archival interventions: participatory research and public historical geographies' https://www.sciencedirect.com/science/article/pii/S0305748814001017

This chapter highlights several points that we might reflect upon. It indicates some direct connections between the past and present through Bressey's more active involvement with a community intent on providing an anti-racist history from below.

Her active involvement with the Black Cultural Archives is discussed here. In reflecting on this paper, you may wish to consider the following:

- Bressey notes links with participatory historical geographies – what do you understand by this idea?
- Bressey links her approach to an idea of 'history from below' – what does this suggest in terms of how we might characterise historical geography and the potential for researching marginalised community histories?
- Bressey highlights funding pressures for archives and museums. How might this impact the documentation and presentation of the past?

ARCHIVES OF THE PRESENT – GEOPOLITICS AND PRESERVING THE PAST IN PRESENT

Donald Trump was President of the United States, for the first time, between 2017 and 2021. When leaving office, there were many questions for geopolitical thinkers in terms of both his legacy and political future. Questions that remain prominent as we write this book following his second inauguration in early 2025. But one aspect of his first tenure might have slipped your attention. At the end of his presidency, White House record keepers began to raise concerns about the state of records held from this time. Numerous letters and correspondence, including communications between Trump and Russian President Vladimir Putin, were reported as either not appropriately filed, kept in a damaged form or perhaps even destroyed. *The Guardian* (2021, n.p.) reported on the challenges faced by the staff responsible for filing and documenting the records of his presidency:

> "My director came up to me and said, 'You have to tape these together,'" said Solomon Lartey, a former White House records analyst. [...]
>
> In the Trump White House "not only has record-keeping not been a priority, but we have multiple examples of it seeking to conceal or destroy that record", said Richard Immerman, from the Society for Historians of American Foreign Relations.

We shouldn't assume that this is something unique to this particular presidency or time period. More recently, there was considerable concern that former British Prime Minister Boris Johnson had seemingly lost over 5000 WhatsApp messages that were pertinent to the COVID-19 inquiry. In the future, this correspondence, which might have provided crucial insights in political decision making during a global pandemic, will not be available. There will be gaps in the archival record and this possibility for fragmented versions of the past has long been recognised by scholars. Whether deliberate or otherwise, the past is continually being constructed and how this is being done will undoubtedly impact the construction of history in the future. How historical geographers might grapple with archival absences then is a key question. What are the limits of what can be said about the past and how might we fill in some of these archival gaps? Chapters 3 and 4 consider these methodological questions in greater detail but for now we foreground contemporary stories of archival creation in the present to pose questions of how one revisits archives of the past.

How is the past retained and remembered? Even when materials are retained carefully and archived for the future, questions of accessibility become prominent. Again, these matters are of geopolitical importance, with questions of ownership of historical objects regularly questioned. History matters in terms of identity, whether national, regional or local and as human geographers we are interested in this layering of the past and its influence in the present. In late 2023 for example, the Greek Prime Minister's visit to Britain received considerable media attention due to his comments around the Parthenon Sculptures, also known as the Elgin Marbles. The marble sculptures date from Ancient Greece and are over 2000 years old. They are currently held at the British Museum. Speaking on the issue in 2023, The Greek Prime Minister, Kyriakos Mitsotakis, claimed that:

> We will never recognise that these sculptures are owned, legally owned by the British Museum … But again, we have to be constructive and we have to be innovative if a solution is to be found.
> (*The Independent*, 2023, n.p.)

His comments during a visit to the United Kingdom reportedly resulted in a cancelled meeting with British Prime Minister Rishi Sunak. More broadly, they posed a series of questions around the appropriate holding location for historical material. As is discussed below, there are many questions here regarding access, but also questions around the violence of removing objects, materials and documents from their place of origin and then questions of return. Such accounts point us towards geopolitical histories which have long fascinated historical geographers. There is scope here to think through the power relations of construction the past, but also the potential for interest in the politics of governance as well as political campaigning. How are people governed through particular time periods, how is society controlled and coerced, and how are matters of social justice brought to the fore? (Figure 1.3).

Questions around provenance, archival presence and absence are considered further in Chapter 3. Your sources might not have been shaped by the decisions of a President but it is highly like that somebody, somewhere, made a decision to retain or destroy a trace of the past you are exploring. Our research is shaped by these decisions, whether politically motivated or not, and this requires acknowledgement and critical reflection when we consider historical geography methods. These processes have long been theorised by geographers and other scholars interested in the construction of pasts. The book reflects in detail on these different perspectives and offers some insight into how you might contend with these challenges. These challenges then should also be part of your thinking in terms of how you write historical geographies and to what extent you are able to

Figure 1.3 Elgin Marbles – provenance, geography and ownership.
Source: Shutterstock: Dennis Diatel.

capture the past through the sources available. These questions are raised at several points in this text and are particularly pertinent to methodological reflections but also consideration of how we might narrate and shape our historical geographies.

COLONIAL HISTORIES/DECOLONIAL FUTURES: KENYA AND 'OPERATION LEGACY'

The two examples above point towards contemporary examples of where historical geography has shown its continued relevance within the public realm. Whether a statue in an urban environment or geopolitical leaders interfering with the recording of their tenure, historical geographies are continually being made and remade. Our final reflective insight in this introduction chapter points to a slightly earlier time period and the practices of colonial administration and their links to documenting the past. It raises similar questions of archival practice and power relations in both recording and accessing the past. Here, we briefly raise how in 2013, 500 elderly Kenyans were awarded £19.9 million in compensation for the violences they

suffered at the hands of British colonialism. Their campaign for justice centred upon the imprisonment, torture and abuse of anti-colonialists, predominantly the Kenyan Mau Mau, who fought for the
independence of Kenya. These historical geographies have a close
connection to the wider work of human geography, connecting
with ongoing attempts to theorise and understand postcolonial and
decolonial practices.

The story is a deeply troubling one but the campaign for justice
ended up uncovering a much wider practice of British colonial
administrators interfering with the historical record. A key part of
the campaign for justice centred upon historical documents from the
time, which reflected some of the abuses in the 1950s. In researching
the case, lawyers and academics worked across Kenya, Britain and
the United States to uncover evidence that could be used in court.
As part of this research, a collection of never-before-seen papers
were unearthed. These records were held secretly by the Foreign
and Commonwealth Office and reflected Colonial Office interventions in several British colonies, particularly during times preceding
independence. Shohei Sato (2017) has revisited the archive creation
from this time and noted how the Colonial Office monitored closely
the processes around administrative documents as independent
nations were in their emergence. The Colonial Office wrote about
this in 1962, specifically for Kenya, but as Sato (2017: 702) points
out this shaped a directive aimed at other territories too, and that the
following principles should be followed for the disposal of classified
and accountable documents:

a. might embarrass Her Majesty's Government or other governments;
b. might embarrass the members of the Police, military forces, pub-
    lic servants or others (such as Police agents or informers);
c. might compromise sources of intelligence;
d. might be used unethically by Ministers in the successor government

These guidelines encouraged the destruction of records, whilst
other materials made their way back to the metropole and were held
in secret. Their uncovering was one of great historical controversy
with wide ranging relevance, including documents relating to the
abuse found in Kenya. The story is covered in a 2018 documentary
entitled *Operation Legacy*, the name also given to the project by the

Colonial Office which destroyed and hid files from the 1950s onwards. As a result of the campaigning efforts, many of those documents that were once inaccessible are now available at the National Archives in London, after the British Government declassified approximately 20,000 files. Clearly, though, those that were destroyed will never be available.

This final example shares much in common with the earlier examples, in terms of archival power and thinking more critically about how the past is assembled and presented, but this example and the wider Operation Legacy poses a further question regarding archival access. These archives remain within Britain. They require a visit to the National Archives in London which is clearly not easily accessible to all. Some documents might be available digitally but again there is a level of resource and knowledge required to begin accessing these records. As this example begins to highlight, documenting and accessing the past becomes far more complex, with a diverse set of geographies, than what we might first assume.

BOX 1.5 Exercise – Thinking like an historical geographer

Having begun to learn about what historical geographies might incorporate, we ask you again to consider what topics in historical geography might be of interest to you? Similarly, you might reflect upon where else have you encountered the past? The prompts below look to connect your earlier research interests with how they are encountered in the present.

- The idea of the role of the past in the present, as well as archives and the power relations associated with documenting the past is introduced above. Consider how histories have been displayed in environments familiar to you? Perhaps a library, archive or museum, or perhaps more public forms of history in the form of a statue, plaque or broader landscape?
- Who has produced these historical presences or narratives? What stories are presented? Are there narratives and perspectives that are perhaps missing?
- What are the stories, who are their audiences, and how are they utilised? Have these histories been contested in any way? How might their meaning have change over time?

Given these more thematic entry points, you may well have rethought your initial responses to the opening exercise. Perhaps you remain interested in your initial suggestion and might now reflect further on how it connects to historical geography. Alternatively, these opening examples might have prompted a new interest or something you hadn't previously considered. The questions above (Box 1.5) are further prompts to help you towards constructing a historical geography idea. We will offer more detailed examples from our own research and the work of others throughout the book, but these early prompts offer you an opportunity to reflect upon your own interests. In what follows, we recognise the limits of our reading of historical geography and our own positionality. This book is not an exhaustive list of everything historical geography might be. Instead, it reflects our own experiences and readings from with the sub-discipline. As such, we provide some brief detail on our positionality and research interests and encourage you to read beyond our own interpretations.

WHO ARE THE AUTHORS?

As co-authors, we come to this book with our own historical geography experiences. These undoubtedly shape the text and our insights likely produce some omissions in our accounting of such a broad sub-discipline. To reflect on this, and to acknowledge our positionality, we briefly provide some details on who we are and how we came into contact with historical geography.

Dr Cheryl McGeachan is a Senior Lecturer in Human Geography at the University of Glasgow. She specialises in the historical geographies of mental ill-health, including exploration of issues of crime, conflict and incarceration. She has written extensively on 'doing' historical geography, particularly through participatory and fragmentary perspectives. She teaches 'Historical Geographies of Care, Conflict and Confinement' at the University of Glasgow and has supervised several historical geography PhD students. Her work can be found in journals such as *Progress in Human Geography*, *Annals of the Association of American Geographers*, the *Journal of Historical Geography* and *Area*.

Dr Paul Griffin is an Assistant Professor in Human Geography at Northumbria University. He teaches 'Historical Geographies: Hidden Histories and Usable Pasts' as part of the BA Geography degree programme. This book reflects some of the themes and topics covered as part of the module. His work connects to historical geography in several ways. He has worked methodologically with archives and oral histories, and holds a particular interest in the idea of 'history from below' and working-class histories. His research has covered labour histories from the early twentieth century, as well as histories of racialised violence. Most recently, he has conducted research around ideas of resistance and solidarity in relation to deindustrialisation and unemployment. These works have been published in journals such as *Area, Antipode, Political Geography* and *Transactions of the Institute of British Geographers*.

In writing this book, we recognise that our reading of historical geography emerges from a particular vantage point. We are both UK-based academics and members of the Historical Geography Research Group within the Royal Geographical Society. We share similar training (having both studied at the University of Glasgow) and are predominantly reliant upon an anglophone reading of historical geography. This places a limit upon the reading of a discipline that stretches beyond these geographies (see Ferretti, 2019) and we recognise that our framing of historical geography comes with limitations. As such, the book should be read not as an exhaustive list of everything historical geography is, but instead as a series of prompts and suggestions for what it might be for particular researchers and audiences. For example, the most recent International Conference of Historical Geography took place in Shanghai in July 2025 showcasing the vibrancy of Chinese historical geography, whilst recent contributions to the *Journal of Historical Geography* and *Geography Compass* increasingly reflect a wide international base to the discipline (Ruohong, Xiaohong and Shuang, 2025; Xu, 2023). We encourage the reader to explore terrains that are familiar or are of interest to them, taking our reflections as prompts for considering diverse historical geographies.

We also hold our own personal connections to practising historical geography. For one of the authors (Griffin), this interest was inspired by an interest in place-based political identities. The initial prompt for exploring the past was found through an interest in contemporary labour struggles in Glasgow, UK, and particularly a curiosity into why particular places held a strong sense of working-class political culture. This contemporary interest, in place-based political identities, quite quickly revealed a need to consider the connections between past and present. Put simply, there was a sense that the struggles of the past informed the culture of the present. From there, I began visiting local archives and discovered a world (for more on 'archives as worldmaking' see Hodder and Krishnan, 2025) of political organising, activists and direct actions, such as the 40 hours movement of 1919. This quickly fascinated me and from there I've continued to use a variety of archives and libraries relating to working class and political left histories. More recently, I have also begun to conduct oral histories to record more recent histories through engagements with memory. All of these engagements have been shaped by a theoretical underpinning from human geography (including terms such as place, space, labour, solidarity, agency, etc.) reflecting on how key ideas and concepts might be connected with past events and lives. It is perhaps this element that has fascinated me most – tracing connections between pasts, presents and futures.

For the other author here (McGeachan), their personal connection to historical geography lies in a fascination with stories and the power they hold to reveal marginalised worlds of experience. My interests in where things begin has always drawn me to the past and as I began to explore the lived worlds of mental ill-health I looked for ways in which to investigate connections across time and place. A key resource for this work has always been archives of different kinds, ranging from institutional, university and museum collections, to personal archives scattered in attics, gardens and rubbish bins. I am captivated by what remains of a life and what stories we can tell (or may never tell) about lives lived and lost. As my work has developed, I have become interested in the ways that we engage with archives to tell stories of experience and have worked in collaboration with experts by experience in communities, prisons and mental health institutions to critically explore ways of working, storying and displaying the past. My theoretical compass is forever evolving; however, my work remains deeply embedded in human geography drawing on concepts such as space, place, memory, power and (in)justice. Working within the realms of historical geography has allowed my work to deeply consider the importance of understanding the lived geographies of people experiencing mental ill-health and why they matter to our wider reflections on what it means to be human. Being able to focus in on such geographies and to trace these across time forges connections between people and place that are missing in other areas of studies and have become a key driving force for my work.

Our motivation for writing this book emerged from a series of conversations regarding our shared teaching experiences. We both teach historical geographies and have generally viewed ourselves as historical geographers in-the-making, through attempts to widen our understanding of what it might mean to use geographical ideas in the past. This book reflects our conversations but also those with wider collaborators, including academics, students, archivists and wider publics. Historical geography perhaps works best when framed as a collaborative endeavour – historical geographies – and this book certainly reflects our passion and drive to work in collaborative, connected and generative ways. Whilst drawing upon our own work and research interests to give a sense of us as engaged practitioners, we have mostly attempted to foreground a wider range of historical geography scholarship that has inspired us and the fields we work within. We view this as a continually evolving exercise and would encourage any reader to read beyond our suggestions.

SUGGESTED READING

Towards the end of each chapter, we provide a short list of focussed reading that might help you address the subjects discussed. A longer bibliography with all the texts cited is available at the end of the chapter.

Clayton, D. (2024) Critical historical geography. Available online: https://www.oxfordbibliographies.com/display/document/obo-9780199874002/obo-9780199874002-0281.xml. Last accessed: 8/11/2024

Cole, T. (2023) 'After the fall, where?: Relocating the Colston statue in Bristol, from 2020 to imaginary futures', *Journal of Historical Geography*, 82, pp. 156–168.

Williamson, B. (2023) 'Historical geographies of place naming: Colonial practices and beyond', *Geography Compass*, 17(5), e12687.

Withers, C.W.J., Domosh, M. and Heffernan, M. (2021) 'Introduction', in Withers, C.W.J., Domosh, M. and Heffernan, M. (eds.) *The SAGE handbook of historical geography*. London: Sage, p. xxvii–L.

CONCLUSIONS AND BOOK STRUCTURE

This opening chapter has sought to introduce historical geographies as a growing sub-discipline of wide-ranging relevance. We have given some detail to the longer history of historical geography, recognising different traditions and approaches and key moments in shaping what we might now consider as an established sub-discipline of historical geography. We have also stressed the variety of approaches and research interests that are found within it. These will be discussed further in the book where we will give more space to explore these varied research interests. The chapter then moved towards some contemporary entry points that shed light on the continued relevance and usability of historical geography. These raise questions of social justice, ethics, archival absences and how might the past be used in the present. They also suggest the continued relevance of the past as we intend to encourage throughout this book.

In what follows, the chapters take different 'cuts' into historical geography, offering a variety of perspectives that will help you to understand the sub-discipline and provide tools for establishing, researching and understanding historical geography research. As such, the chapters are framed around the process of generating research. The following chapter reflects upon 'sparking curiosity' and builds upon the early entry points of this chapter to suggest what historical geography might be. We move beyond the general entry points offered here and begin to focus more on the spatial approach emphasised within the sub-discipline, drawing more closely upon historical geography scholarship to indicate the vibrant possibilities for your own research.

Following this, Chapter 3 takes a closer look at historical geography methods, reflecting more closely on the use of archives as a method to engage with the past. The chapter reflects upon the question of historical absence as a challenge we all must grapple with. The notion of 'working with fragments' is considered to reflect upon the challenges of engaging with *what remains*. Chapter 4 considers the question of *where is the geography*? In answering this prompt, the chapter stresses the importance of applying key concepts and ideas to an exploration of the past. A thorough grounding in the application of key concepts and ideas within historical geography is given in this chapter through attention to a wide geographical and temporal range of examples from throughout the literature, for example post-structural, postcolonial and feminist perspectives.

Chapter 5 considers the practicalities of working with historical materials. It reflects on this through two particular examples, relating to the authors' work, showcasing the range of ways in which different types and forms of historical materials can be worked with in historical geography research. Exercises that highlight key skills including interpretation, coding and analysis are discussed in order to generate an understanding of the varying ways in which historical materials can be used and worked through. Chapter 6 builds upon the analysis to reflect on the act of writing historical geographies. This chapter will chart the various ways in which historical geography can be written through discussion of examples in the sub-field. It will also consider some of the more practical elements related to writing pasts. Aspects of critical writing and creative writing will be showcased and exercises given that will enable and inspire the reader to try out particular styles and formats in relation to their ideas and research areas.

Our concluding chapter draws together our reflections across the book. It does so by proposing what we describe as a *manifesto for historical geography*. Here, we pose some critical questions for historical geographies of the future, whilst also inviting the reader to consider the most pressing challenges for the sub-discipline. This chapter conveys the important juncture for historical work in the present, highlighting the significance for understanding the past to tackle core issues of inequality and injustice. Portraying historical geography work as a tool for promoting more hopeful futures, the concluding chapter outlines a manifesto for historical geography that seeks to inspire readers to develop their own work and to think carefully and creatively about it in terms of the possibilities for wider impacts.

REFERENCES

Clayton, D. (2024) Critical historical geography. *Oxford Bibliographies*. Available online: https://www.oxfordbibliographies.com/display/document/obo-9780199874002/obo-9780199874002-0281.xml. Last accessed: 8/11/2024.

Cole, T. (2023) 'After the fall, where?: Relocating the Colston statue in Bristol, from 2020 to imaginary futures', *Journal of Historical Geography*, 82, pp. 156–168.

Cresswell, T. (2024) *Geographic thought: A critical introduction.* Hoboken, NJ: Wiley Blackwell.

Ding, Y. (2021) 'Decentralisation of historical geography in China 2006–2020', *Geography Compass*, p. e12550.

Ferretti, F. (2019) 'Rediscovering other geographical traditions', *Geography Compass*, 13(3), p. e12421.

Griffin, P. (2018) 'Making usable pasts: Collaboration, labour and activism in the archive', *Area*, 50(4), pp. 501–508.

Heffernan, M. (2009). 'Historical geography'. In Gregory, D., Johnston, R., Pratt, G., Watts, M. and Whatmore., S. (eds.), *The dictionary of human geography*. Fifth edn. Oxford: Wiley-Blackwell, pp. 332–5.

Hodder, J. and Krishnan, S. (2025) 'Archives as worldmaking', *Journal of Historical Geography*, 88, pp. 39–42.

Mitchell, J.B. (1954) *Historical geography*. London: English Universities Press.

Ruohong, L., Xiaohong, Z. and Shuang, L. (2025) 'Characteristics and trends in Chinese historical geography (2019–2024)', *Journal of Historical Geography*, 88, pp. 17–26.

Sato, S. (2017) "Operation Legacy": Britain's destruction and concealment of colonial records worldwide', *The Journal of Imperial and Commonwealth History*, 45(4), pp. 697–719.

The Guardian (2021) Historians having to tape together records that Trump tore up. *The Guardian*. Available from: https://www.theguardian.com/us-news/2021/jan/17/historians-having-to-tape-together-records-that-trump-tore-up. Last accessed 6/3/2024.

The Independent (2023) We want win-win solution on Elgin Marbles, says Greek prime minister. *The Independent*. Available from: https://www.independent.co.uk/news/world/europe/greece-elgin-marbles-uk-museum-athens-b2337904.html. Last accessed: 14/4/2025.

Williamson, B. (2023) 'Historical geographies of place naming: Colonial practices and beyond', *Geography Compass*, 17(5), p. e12687.

Withers, C.W.J., Domosh, M. and Heffernan, M. (2021) 'Introduction'. In Withers, C. W. J., Domosh, M. and Heffernan, M. (eds) *The SAGE handbook of historical geography*. London: Sage, p. xxvii–L.

Xu, Y. (2023) 'Historical geographies of Japanese colonial urbanism', *Geography Compass*, p. e12717.

2

SPARKING CURIOSITY

INTRODUCTION

Chapter 1 encouraged you to follow your own interests and provided a series of prompts to begin to situate these within historical
geography. This chapter picks up the baton from Chapter 1 and
steers the reader towards a more sustained engagement with historical
geography as research in practice. It does so to situate your own historical geography research in relation to existing disciplinary trends
and approaches. As such, there is a clearer focus here upon researching historical geography and a closer engagement with scholarship at
the forefront of the sub-discipline. In doing so, the chapter offers a
distinctive take on what historical geography might mean for you.
The title reflects this by indicating that the aim of the chapter is to
spark a research curiosity. It might be that this connects with the
earlier prompts provided but it might also be that your interests are
still yet to emerge. Either is fine at this stage, as overall, the chapter
aims to provide a clearer sense of how historical geography might
provide an entry point for your interests and engagements.

To do so, the chapter is structured around three geographical
scales. It moves between a more intimate portrayal of microhistories,
towards place-based narratives and then more global and connected
historical geographies. These are scalar devices that are useful for
showing the distinctive nature of historical geography. Although
they should not be read as discrete modes of historical geography
inquiry. Indeed, as will be noted through some concluding remarks,
it is possible to find the global within the micro, and the micro and
intimate within the global. As such, the scales introduced are used

DOI: 10.4324/9781003483588-2

here as a method to stress the geography of the approach taken towards the past. Their emphasis upon space, place and relational understandings steers the researcher towards a critical geography of historical events, experiences and lives. Before delving further into these particular scales of historical geography, the chapter offers some broader reflections on historical geography directions. It does so to introduce the breadth of historical geography and the potential research interests which might inspire your approach towards the past. These entry points are wide-ranging and conceptually driven, something which is picked up further in Chapter 4, and are the first sparks of curiosity offered.

Following this emphasis upon breadth, the chapter moves towards the three scales of inquiry previously mentioned. The section structured around micro-historical geographies considers smaller spaces of interest, including prisons, asylums, ships and the home as sites where geographers have utilised close engagement with the intimate to shape and extend understandings of wider social phenomena. The next section extends the scope of engagement towards a wider place-based or regional approach, one that extends the scale away from the most intimate and towards an approach which might characterise a wider site, such as city, town or region. Several examples are drawn upon here, including the histories of deindustrialisation, rural historical geographies and more broadly approaches to understanding landscape. The final scalar section looks towards a more mobile, connected and ultimately global sense of historical geography. It draws upon examples relating to seafarers, migration, solidarities and anti-war struggles to illustrate a more relational and connected sense of historical geography. A key argument across the sections is that the tools of the historical geographer allow a more relational understanding of the past, and that there is scope to blend differing modes of analysis.

WHERE MIGHT HISTORICAL GEOGRAPHY TAKE YOU?

As suggested in Chapter 1, historical geography is a vibrant, diverse and ever-changing sub-discipline. The research found within associated scholarship covers many subject areas. They are held together through their engagement with the past but do so in quite different ways. Before introducing a scalar approach, this chapter briefly introduces some thematic entry points which might act as an early prompt for your research. It does so by surveying some of the emerging historical geography research which best reflects this exciting and ever-changing field of research. The list is not exhaustive but does give some sense of emerging trends and ways of thinking.

Most recently, scholars have taken forward the challenge of addressing societal challenges and inequalities. The changing nature of historical geography, as introduced in Chapter 1, has pushed historical geographers to question their research subjects and research approaches. Two trends are particularly noteworthy here, firstly feminist historical geographies and secondly decolonial approaches. These approaches, unpacked below, have pushed historical geographers to address the absences, power relations and exclusions within representations of the past. In particular, they attend to the geographies of gender as found within the past and similarly a critical revisiting of historical geographies through a greater recognition of colonial forces and the voices and perspectives which are hidden or silenced. From a decolonial perspective, it is absolutely crucial that these voices are widened, and alternative perspectives are heard. Some brief reflections are given with regards to these critical insights before wider thinking is offered. This is considered important to reflect historical geography as a dynamic sub-discipline that is continually shaped and developed by both scholars and society.

Feminist historical geography has been described by Briony McDonagh (2018, p. 1564) as:

> scholarship which asks geographical questions of historical material and is informed by feminist theories, approaches and methodologies. Its empirical subject matter is necessarily expansive and diverse, but often has a particular focus on the lives of women and other marginalized groups, and on the ways gender and space were – and are – co-constituted.

This approach has been characterised by an attentiveness to women's lives but also a focus upon gendered relations (how the concept of gender shapes, influences and is shaped by spatial processes). In doing so, it has addressed missing voices from more dominant historical narratives, for example, reflections on the ways in which wives of colonial administrators might reveal the dynamics of gender as found within the intimate historical geographies of colonial territories. Similarly, feminist historical geography has emphasised the role of women's activisms in resisting societal injustices, including but not limited by, those related to gendered discrimination. More broadly, the approach is indicative of how a theoretically informed approach might drive engagements with the archive. Here, associated researchers utilise ideas from feminist theory to revisit the past, and as such attend to particular elements of the archival record and represent this in dialogue with ongoing theoretical conversations (more on this in Chapter 4).

In similar terms, decolonial approaches have asked important questions of historical geography. Decolonial endeavours are characterised by a more proactive engagement to address contemporary injustices associated with colonialism. Such efforts include revisiting pasts, reflecting on how the past is curated in the present, and moving towards anti-racist and more socially just futures. These works are driven by anti-racist theorising and look to draw upon a wider range of scholarship, particularly those of a wider geography, including Black geographies and indigenous communities within the places we might write about. As Sarah Radcliffe describes, decolonial approaches encourage scholars to recognise how:

> British geography is characterised by its whiteness among academic staff and undergraduate students; decolonising geography socially and institutionally is hence an uphill struggle to confront and dismantle the 'unbearable whiteness of geography' (Derickson, 2017: p.236).
>
> (Radcliffe, 2017, p. 331)

Such a challenge to the discipline has had a far-reaching influence, not only shaping historical geography, but more broadly influencing how academic and other institutions grapple with their links to colonial pasts and imagine anti-racist and progressive futures. In response, historical geographers have increasingly engaged with a wider range of perspectives and geographies. These include the histories of anti-colonial struggles, identifying actors and organising practices that attempted not only to resist colonial rule but also imagine a world beyond that too. Similarly, scholars have looked to provide a more global sense of what historical geography means by identifying the contributions of historical geographers in countries beyond those dominated by anglophone worlds (Ferretti, 2019). Doing so begins to address power imbalances embedded within academic institutions, whilst also providing a wider range of empirical settings and theoretical tools for historical geographers to draw upon. There is clearly much more work to be done.

These are just two theoretically informed entry points but the list of potential research subjects for historical geography is far wider. The importance of theory is picked up in greater depth in Chapter 4. To give some sense of the variety related to this, it is worth noting that historical geographers have been prominent contributors to scholarship on a range of research subjects, including science and exploration, noting in particular the role of geography in shaping the boundaries and borders of the world (Williamson, 2023), but also reflecting on the changing scientific tradition with reflections around the role of technology as well as key practitioners (Naylor, 2005). Alongside this, military historical geography has revisited military conflict to uncover new stories from the battlefield, including those during World Wars. Isla Forsyth (2012), for example, reflects on the evolving role of camouflage through close engagement with the scientific biography of Dr Hugh Cott. Beyond this, historical geographers have looked closely at mental health, race and racism, and institutional geographies more broadly, tracing changing approaches towards understanding governmentality and changing approaches towards societal difference. Alongside these societal constraints, historical geographers have been at the forefront of reflecting upon practices of solidarity and resistance (Awcock, 2021; Featherstone, 2012), revealing alternative world views and the persistent presence of contesting voices. These brief insights showcase some of the varied potential of historical geography to complement the two theoretical positions introduced above and provide some of the more empirical interests so far pursued.

Some suggested entry points and subject areas to engage with are identified in Table 2.1. What will become clear is that to engage with these sorts of subject matters a wider reading list beyond geography is required. Historical geographers are known for wide ranging, often inter-disciplinary, approaches. What follows next, is a

Table 2.1 Reading historical geographies – some disciplinary areas and trends.

Subject Area	Histories
Feminist historical geographies	Gendered relations, home, women's activisms, women's lives
Decolonial approaches	Independence movements, anticolonial movements, race, racism and anti-racism, black geographies
Science and exploration	Colonial explorations, science and geography, technology, social difference and science
Environmental historical geographies	Histories of environmental change, historical disasters, participatory historical geography, histories of community adaptation
Military histories	Conflict, battlefields, death, injury, military art
Institutional historical geographies	Prisons, asylums, schools, governmentality
Understanding landscape	Rural, urban, labour, deindustrialisation, rewilding
Historical geographies of resistance, and solidarity	Protest, trade unions, social justice movements, community organising

closer reading of specific contributions structured around the scales previously mentioned, moving from the micro to the global. These scalar engagements begin to reveal the wide variety of research interests, whilst also more closely engaging with the geographies revealed in the work. We begin with the most intimate scale of analysis and move outwards towards more globally connected histories.

MICRO-HISTORICAL GEOGRAPHIES

Our scalar entry point is one found within the most intimate modes of geographical inquiry. Here we suggest that there is great potential for historical geographers to examine the micro, to work with smaller moments and spaces, as well as writing more intimate experiences and attending to intricacy. There has been a wide range of historical geography research that has centred small spaces. Here the notion of 'small' is flexible but does indicate a focus upon something more intimate than the following modes of inquiry. Whether it be through attention to a home, room, hospital ward or prison cell, or through a spatial approach to include intimate experiences, including friendships, comradery or even more hateful, violent relationships, historical geographers have illustrated how intimacy might reveal something wider about the relationships between society and space. In doing so, the sub-discipline has built upon a wider tradition also found within history, that of micro-history, which Magnusson (no date) describes as:

> The microhistorians placed their emphasis on small units and how people conducted their lives within them. By reducing the scale of observation, microhistorians argued that they are more likely to reveal the complicated function of individual relationships within each and every social setting and they stressed its difference from larger norms. Micohistorians tend to focus on *outliers* rather than looking for the *average* individual as found by the application of quantitative research methods.

Taking this as our starting point we can begin to reveal the work of historical geographers that might resonate most with this approach. These historical geographers have paid close attention to smaller details, the nuances and particularities of small spaces. In doing so, they might reveal connections with wider forces and processes, but the emphasis here lies upon the intimate. There are many examples we could foreground and several are offered below: prison spaces, asylums, the home, the body and the ship.

Author, Cheryl McGeachan's (2018) research on carceral spaces has drawn attention to a relatively small space within a larger prison site. Her work links with the role of prisons as institutions and more broadly the growing sub-discipline of carceral geography. She considers an experimental approach to penal reform within a Glasgow prison in the 1970s exploring records associated with the Barlinnie Special Unit, which was an experimental therapeutic initiative with violent prisoners in 1973. The experiment catalysed a series of measures which disrupted the carceral space and introduced some forms of freedom:

> The Special Unit was housed within Barlinnie Prison, located in the residential suburb of Riddrie in the North-East of Glasgow. The experimental design of the Unit was showcased in its

architecture and the spatial arrangements put in place to encourage the development of therapeutic community principles.

Prisoners were able to move freely around the unit, utilising the spaces in ways that were deemed appropriate by the "community." For example, in a typical day, prisoners' cells were open from 6 a.m. to 9 p.m., with free access to spaces such as the outside yard and the kitchen area where prisoners made their own arrangements regarding cooking and making coffee.

(McGeachan, 2018, p. 203)

Her archival research considers the project both through the institutional ideas of the prison and spatial tactics associated with prison reform, but also through the worlds and perspectives of the prisoners and prison workers themselves. A social reformer who was part of the experiment reflected on their experiences of the prison cell and the sense of pride and ownership offered through personalisation:

Each cell becomes a little world, the only space in which the inmate has privacy. Each cell is decorated according to the individual taste by its occupant. As with any home an unwritten code of behaviour operates.

(Carmichael, 1982 cited in McGeachan, 2018, p. 204)

At the same time, some prisoners felt uncomfortable with the shift in roles, and were unable to adjust to the new freedom. Similarly, the changes introduced continued to be limited in light of larger structural processes. Prisoners were still held within the prison and were subjected to carceral structures, albeit in a significantly altered form. It is these dynamics that the research attends to. The experiment gives an insight into the lived worlds of carceral spaces (Figure 2.1). This has become an increasing interest for human geographers, with the work of carceral geography in particular becoming increasingly influential in how prison spaces are conceptualised and offering critical insights for future prison policy (see Moran, 2015).

Historical geography research has contributed significantly to this sub-field, by foregrounding engagements with prison practices and drawing attention to different spatial dynamics as found within prisons. Indeed, the quotes above describe prison cells themselves as a 'little world,' something which geographers might wish to

Figure 2.1 Prison space – a site of historical and carceral geography.

Source: Shutterstock: Nicole Piepgras.

explore further. The scalar perspective of narrowing in on not just a prison, but a particular unit and at times particular cells, offers great insight into the variable dynamics found within prison walls. As indicated above, the Special Unit offered additional freedoms that were rehabilitative for some yet remained unfamiliar and uncomfortable for others. Returning to the analytical work of McGeachan, she frames these experiences as sitting at the nexus of care and control. Her research elaborates on the brief insights provided above to reveal a nuanced sense of the dynamics of prison-staff interactions where particular acts might not always be easily delineated as either care or control. Perhaps those acts intended to care might also be viewed through a lens of control, and vice versa. It is within these nuances that research such as this becomes most revealing.

A similar dynamic of care and control might also be identified within the historical geographies of mental (ill-)health. Chris Philo for example, has shown how the emergence of asylum spaces in nineteenth century England revealed an increasing interest in 'madness' and 'scientific' treatments, as characterised most through the institutional emergence of the Lunatic Asylum. These were, as Foucault (1965, p. 251) described, a 'space reserved by society for insanity.' Their emergence marked a change in how those deemed in need of mental health treatment were institutionalised:

> A vital point in this connection was that most contemporaries believed there to be some relationship between the so-called nineteenth-century 'march of civilization', as epitomized by the spreading urban-industrial landscape of gloomy tenements and smoky factory chimneys, and the production – indeed, according to most statistics, increased production – of insanity.
>
> (Philo, 1987, p. 404)

Lunatic Asylums began to emerge in late eighteenth century England, with York Lunatic Asylum opening in 1777 for example. The subsequent years witnessed substantial growth in the number of asylums and the amount of patients held within their walls. Historic England (n.d) identify how '[i]n 1806, the average asylum housed 115 patients and by 1900 the average was over 1,000.' They also indicate how '[e]arly optimism that people could be cured had vanished. The asylum became simply a place of confinement.' Historical geographers, like Philo, have traced these institutional histories, illustrating a constantly changing approach, informed by increasing levels of scientific intervention, and an emergent pattern in mental health treatment. A significant part of this examination has been to analyse the smaller spaces located within these institutional histories. Examples of these include an analysis of asylum policy, examining the location of an asylum, and exploring its environment and atmospheres. They have shown how every element of these spaces was carefully designed with a similar control/care nexus as indicated above. One small example of this can be found through the preference for a rural location for asylums, which generally reflected the view that removing individuals from industrialising environments might have therapeutic value, but this was deeply contested with the view that this only heightened the sense of isolation and unfamiliarity for those confined within asylum spaces.

In contrast to these institutional geographies, historical geographers have also uncovered past experiences of domestic settings through the geographies of the home. This work again centres upon smaller spaces and units of analysis. Feminist historical geographers have revisited the domestic sphere to illuminate divisions of labour and intimate experiences within the home space. They have revealed unequal distributions of care, emotional labour and gendered roles as found within the geographies of the home. Similarly, the sphere of reproduction has indicated the home as a formative space of child-hood but also as a space of political subjectivity. Historical geogra-phers have showed the home to be a space of political activism, revealing more private relations of politics, including but not limited to women's activisms. Small acts of banner making, demonstration planning and general practices of organising have a long history of taking place within domestic spaces, as well as the larger, more public activisms. The home then is a multifaceted site of historical geography interest.

One empirical example is found within the work of Lloyd and Johnson (2004) who revisit home magazines to consider the chang-ing representations of gender relations in post-war Australia. They engage closely with magazines such as the *Australian Women's Weekly* and the *Australian Home Beautiful* between 1940 and 1960. Their research highlights a shift in post–Second World War representations of domestic settings. They note an important change through increasing public interest in a previously private sphere, and also reflect upon the role of women as represented through these publications:

> We argue through a case study of the figure of the housewife in Australian home magazines that as a result of this contradiction during this period the identity of 'housewife' came to offer a new, reflexive relationship between female selfhood and home. Via the domestication of modernity in terms of gender, previous divi-sions between the public and private were destabilised. We suggest that the housewife's gaze both towards the home and towards her 'domestic self' intensified the problematic of femininity, putting it on the threshold of public and private space, offering a critical, enabling position for an ensuing feminist analysis.
>
> (Lloyd and Johnson, 2004, p. 251)

The magazines reveal a contradiction in that the domestic sphere became of public interest and positioned as part of nation building, with women centred in this approach, yet the agency of women remained constrained. Through engagements with magazines, their work reveals how the home is repositioned through which interior home making is reimagined as a space of nation building. Women were centred in this reimagining, something which might be considered as a significant moment in reflecting the changing geographies of the home, particularly with emerging forms of technological change (that would assist domestic labour), yet at the same time, these changes continued to constrain women's worlds largely within the domestic setting. The study foregrounds a further tension in our thinking through of domestic spaces, as both container of experiences and world making setting, in which women's agency is present but also a site forged in relation to wider spaces and as one that constrains as much as it might enable (Figure 2.2).

Feminist historical geographies have also pushed the discipline further through engagements with the body as site of study. Perhaps

Figure 2.2 Magazines – a source for historical geography/critical analysis.

Source: Shutterstock: Copyright Lawrey.

this reveals the most intimate and micro scale of engagement, whereby embodied experiences are centred. Ana Laura Zavala Guillen (2023), for example, considers the histories of marooned women who escaped slavery in Northern Colombia. The stories themselves are powerful and reveal the hidden histories, and continued struggle, of Afro-Latin America, particularly through territories, such as San Basilo de Palenque, a town developed by fugitives from slavery. Using a variety of archival sources and tracing memories through oral histories with Maroon descendent women, Zavala Guillen's work specifically centres the body as a site through which the historical geographies of territory can be understood, revealing how one particular Maroon descendent woman navigated her current displacement with her own descendance from fugitives. She notes how María de Los Santos continued to return to the lands (La Pista) from which she was displaced:

> On one hand, many men cultivate plots of land there by day, returning to La Pista in the evening, some of them out of fear and others who now say they feel at home in their new spaces. On the other hand, María de Los Santos began to rebuild a space on her old piece of land, seeking to demonstrate to those at La Pista, by way of her intimately remaining at L.B., that the recovery of the Maroon-descendant territories, of which they had been stripped by armed violence, is also a real option. For María de Los Santos, this is better than remaining amid the material precariousness of La Pista, because of its bare subsistence-based economy and extreme poverty.
>
> (Zavala Guillen, 2023, p. 88)

Here she utilises the concept of 'territorio cuerpo-tierra (body-land as territory)' to foreground the embodied ways in which the connections between history, body and territory are lived and felt, particularly within the context of military violence and displacement. In doing so, she identifies the tangible ways in which history is not a detached study of the past, but instead a lived, intimate, embodied dynamic between individuals, communities and their territories. Her retelling of these stories is particularly powerful for stressing the continued resonance of the past in the present, and the ways in which slavery pasts might intersect with contemporary lives and struggles.

Such works are also indicative of the potential to widen our historical geography reading lists, so to include scholarship from Latin America and beyond, and to continually consider anti-colonial and decolonial perspectives.

Finally, in relation to micro-historical geographies, we might also situate a micro engagement with more mobile historical geographies. Indeed, this final example links closely with the global historical geographies section introduced later but does so through the more intimate relations of mobility. Those found within a particular space, that of the ship and through seafaring relations. In this regard, mobility is something that is intimately felt and experienced, something more than travelling from A to B and might instead be understood through the intimacy of travel. The ship offers one vantage point for exploring this, and maritime historical geographers have shed some light on the experiences of the sea as being experienced, felt and lived. Some brief examples are considered here to show the scope of potential engagement with mobility. William Hasty for example has indicated how ships, and particularly the pirate ship:

> existed as a real, lived and dynamic space, one crafted by pirates in their own image with their own ends in mind. The ship functioned as a technology of mobility and speed, as a locale for piratical politics and as a space of multiple contestations, and revealing their spatial practices in modifying this space sheds much needed light on their intriguing way of life.
>
> (Hasty, 2014, p. 364)

Similarly, Markus Rediker suggested that the pirate ship reflected 'the world turned upside down' (Rediker, 2004, p. 61), documenting how pirate captains and workers would often coalesce and work in a co-operative manner. This was in direct contrast to other more hierarchical forms of shipping labour. Hasty was keen to identify the uneven nature of such radical spaces, noting comparisons and differences between pirate ships, whereby some ships would continue to maintain more vertical hierarchical structures (e.g. clear distinguishing of captain space).

The historian Marcus Rediker (2007), used here due to his work's considerable impact on historical geographers such as Hasty, has also shown how within these spaces, humans might experience mobility

BOX 2.1 Exercise – Working with micro-historical geographies

The extract below provides an insight into the Barlinnie Special Unit introduced above. It can be considered a source, offering a personal perspective.

Your task is to read the autobiographical reflection and consider the questions beneath it:

> I was then asked by a screw if I would come round and sort out my personal property with him. I went, and while we opened the parcels containing old clothes he did something that to him was so natural but to me was something that had never been done before. He turned to me and handed me a pair of scissors and asked me to cut open some of them. He then went about his business. I was absolutely stunned. That was the first thing that made me begin to feel human again. It was the completely natural way that it was done. This simple gesture made me think. In my other world, the penal system in general, such a thing would never happen.

(Boyle, 1977, p. 229)

1. The insight above is taken from an autobiography of a former prisoner. How might personal insights extend our understanding of carceral spaces?
2. Focus in on the micro-interactions experienced by Boyle – in what ways is the prison space reimagined here?
3. Are there any links to the care control nexus previously introduced?

differently. Through archival research on the most exploitable conditions imaginable, his work has illustrated how 'small acts' of resistance were found on the seventeenth-century slave ship. In *The Slave Ship: A Human History* he notes how slaves resisted the inhuman conditions, violence and terror of their passage, through acts such as hunger strikes, jumping overboard and insurrections. Similarly, in the context of Cuba, Manuel Barcia (2017, p. 73) has explored how slave suicides operated as a form of resistance, describing how 'every new suicide committed in the island rep-resented an economic loss as well as a signal to the outside world that Cuban slavery was not the "human" system they were trying to portray.'

His study takes a closer look at the historical dynamics and conditions which led to such acts and describes how slaves framed their final act of suicide, through starvation or drowning, in the belief that it marked a 'return home to their own country and friends again.' Rediker considers how these acts might be understood as practices of mutual aid and survival, positioned within 'the beginnings of a culture of resistance, the subversive practices of negotiation and insurrection' (Rediker, 2007, p. 350). Such insights are indicative of the world making spaces onboard ships. They reveal relatively intimate spaces within vast oceans whereby spatial political relations, of exploitation and violence, as well as solidarity and resistance, might come to the fore in our thinking with micro-histories.

PLACE-BASED HISTORICAL GEOGRAPHIES

Moving outwards from these smaller spaces, the chapter now considers what might be best described as a place-based scale of inquiry. Again, this is offered as a flexible approach to revealing what historical geography might be, rather than a rigid scalar definition that installs limits on your approach. Instead, this widening of the geographical scope offers a sense of scale that can characterise place. It offers an approach that engages closely with a particular place, landscape or environment and attempts to characterise it through what might be best thought of as a more aggregated sense of history, building upon the micro-histories introduced previously. To help with this, the *Dictionary of Human Geography* provides some useful opening definitions of what place might mean for geographers:

1. A fixed point on the Earth's surface.
2. A locus of individual and group identity.
3. The scale of everyday life.

> Until the 1970s all three meanings of place were understood via a 'mosaic' metaphor that implied that different places were discrete and singular. However, in the wake of globalization, it became necessary for human geographers to rethink their ideas about place.
>
> (Rogers, Castree and Kitchin, 2013, n.p.)

Some of these definitions are relatively straightforward on the surface but they do also give us some insight for what follows in thinking about place-based historical geographies. They reflect place as location, place as experienced and place as something shared. They also begin to reveal a changing sense of place with added nuance through connections and diversity. One method of engaging with places has been to think about engagement with place through the associated term of landscape(s), identifying histories that inform the sites around us. The shift in language here to include landscape alongside notions of place begins to provide insight into the processual understanding of place, whether that be through cultural meanings, social practices, economic processes or political dynamics. This more relational understanding of place, which has long fascinated geographers, offers alternative approaches in how best to aggregate meanings and how we might write about place and historical geographies.

Three examples follow where the mode of analysis is switched from the micro towards place-based. This shift is a subtle one and some elements might overlap. The analysis starts with two contrasting historical approaches to places and landscapes, first with a close engagement to cultural meaning through collective forms of memory making, and second through comments on the histories of work and migration as embedded within the rural aesthetic. The section then switches to a closer look at urban environments and the dynamics of deindustrialisation as found within place-based historical geographies. These insights are introduced to show the potential for geographers to tie histories to understandings of places, whilst also indicating differences in how we might go about these endeavours.

First, Hayden Lorimer's (2019) encounter with a coastal landscape is grounded in a close engagement with the meaning of place through what he describes as 'lifeworlds.' In reflecting on place-writing, and the potential for deep engagement with a particular site and location, he takes us to a less familiar setting, a relatively remote coastline location in the North of Scotland. More specifically, he reflects on his frequent visits to a pet cemetery and his interactions with the 'keeper' of this site. His writing around this place is a deep rooted one, forged with a personal connection to the site, and is delivered through a deliberately constructed prose of creative non-fiction, capturing the environment he regular frequented as well as continual reflection between observation, place and writing (more on this in Chapter 6). One particularly vivid example is included here as a slightly extended excerpt as it captures the distinctive feel of the approach:

> The burial site is spread across a parcel of reclaimed ground, plots landscaped into gently graduating slopes. When seen from the cliff-top above, or the vantage point afforded by rocks accessible at low tide, the fanned-out shape of a scallop shell is revealed. Closer-to, gravestones confirm what might easily be guessed at: former four-legged friends crowd the scene. The memory of dead dogs: Mac, Max, Clyde, Rex, Buddy, Mutley and Tyson. Almost as many cats jostling for position: a number of Tiddles, several Tiggers, alongside Smokey, Misty, Baby, Princess, Snowflake. And one Pussy Galore. Smaller burial spots keep the cartoon foes apart, in-filled with a carnival of other animals: hamsters, rabbits, tortoises, turtles, budgies, mice, ferrets, guinea pigs and goldfish. There's Coco. Sooty, Skippy and Sandy. Patch and Bracken. Mowgli and Lucky. Ricky. Petra. Finn. Thumper. Yoda. One thousand and one tales of devotion and loss, love and death, embedded within the single story unfolding here.
>
> (Lorimer, 2019, p. 334)

This writing is based upon many visits to the site, as well as some conversations with the Keeper. Lorimer's methodology is informed by ethnographic and oral history methods, capturing place through both cultural and personal meaning. The writing style here is different to the more typical analytical approach found within historical geography, and human geography more broadly. Rather than quickly transitioning from the empirical evidence to theoretical reflection, Lorimer stays with the detail and writes a history of an unfamiliar place through close engagement with the detail. We return to this writing style in more detail in Chapter 6.

In doing so, he is perhaps able to capture some of the less tangible components of place, those more atmospheric and emotional elements of meaning. The listing of pet names for example gives a poignant sense of attachment and loss, something which Lorimer then links to the longer term meaning of the site whereby the local community collectively campaigned for its continuation during a territorial dispute with the landowner. His writing therefore considers how history informs attachments to place, and how these 'life-worlds' prove significant in our making sense of the sites around us. It is these interactions, memories and experiences which gives place meaning and Lorimer is keen for us not to move too quickly away from the immediacy of place. Your own historical geography work might look to do something similar, by more closely tracing the links between place-based pasts (through archives, oral histories and ethnography) and place-based futures (through writing, outputs and more public facing work).

In slight contrast to this, Don Mitchell (1996), takes an alternative approach to understanding landscape through his engagement with the early twentieth century Californian rural landscapes. His analysis is on a wider scale than Lorimer's, as he looks to capture a political economy through the history of place, researching and retelling the stories of migrant workers who shaped the landscape. Rather than viewing the rural landscape as one simply of natural beauty, ripe for artistic representation as a rural idyll, he instead points to the human processes, injustices and resistances, that shaped the landscape. His book *The Lie of the Land* served as an alternative form of landscape writing by identifying how 'landscape geographers have turned in other directions, preferring to explore a politics of representation that is seemingly quite disconnected from issues of labor' (Mitchell, 1996, p. 4).

In response, his work foregrounds the 'continuing history of struggle that has made these landscapes' (Mitchell, 1996, p. 201) and notes the significant role of workers' struggles, particularly those of trade unions, as well as the labour and experiences of Chinese migrant workers in shaping the contemporary landscape. His work is particularly attentive to the histories of migrant workers within these landscapes, with 75 per cent of California's agricultural workers in 1890 from China. These workers laboured under highly exploitative conditions and suffered racism from both above (government) and below (white workers), resulting in eventual exclusion from these labour markets with the Chinese Exclusion Act of 1882. The imprint of Chinese migrant workers on the California landscape, both agriculturally and within cities, is undoubtable, though, with their involvement in the gold rush, farm work and the construction of the transcontinental railroad crucial in the regional development as well as the changing rural landscape. Drawing attention to this history of migration and work, alongside other workers' struggles for social justice, remains central to Mitchell's efforts to characterise the landscapes of California. These perspectives could be easily missed if researchers were not able to attend to the historical geographies of work and migration. These nuances might therefore be lost in an account towards place which reads it only at surface level. Mitchell's work points towards an understanding of labour relations as significant for thinking through the history of place and resonates with other places too. A similar analysis might be applied to the relationship between processes of deindustrialisation and understanding place-based historical geographies.

This third insight into thinking through place, is marked by a significant social-economic shift caused by industrial closures and has been widely studied by historical geographers. Often recognised as a contextual factor for contemporary political times, historical geography has been at the forefront of studying the impacts of deindustrialisation. These detailed studies of the economic, emotional and cultural impact of societal change have shown the relationship between work, place and society. Jay Emery foregrounds working class experiences in his theorisation of deindustrialisation, place-based histories and emotions. He centres his engagements in the Nottinghamshire coalfields to reveal how the impacts of job losses, community change and legacies of mining continue to have influence in multifaceted ways. He points to how:

> Processes and 'legacies' of deindustrialisation and postindustrialism over the last few decades have disrupted and confused these supposedly once stable formations. The shift toward labour markets based on services, combined with the trauma of job losses and deindustrialisation, has resulted in a mourning for lost ways of life and work. These senses of loss endure in bodies, materialities and memories and, it is suggested, have provoked a pervasive nostalgia within deindustrialised communities.
>
> (Emery, 2018, pp. 79–80)

Other emotions are pertinent here too with studies revealing the sense of loss, nostalgia and memory in remembering places as they used to be. Emery is similarly keen to explore nuance understandings of these processes to stress how they might be experienced differently, introducing connections to the geographies of gender and race, and intersecting these with the stress upon working class communities. Engagements with memory have been central to this approach, with oral histories commonly used to gain insights into the relationships between past and present within post-industrial societies. Similarly, scholars have been keen to point out the persistent presence of alternative narratives and community forms of solidarity and resistance

BOX 2.2 Exercise – Working with place-based experiences

The theme of deindustrialisation is raised above. This process is a complex one and is experienced differently by different people in different places. The account below emerges in 1980s Britain. It documents the experience of a recently unemployed man in Newcastle, England. Regional unemployment in the 1980s reached over 16% in the North East of England. The extract below comes from a trade unionist reflecting on their own period of job loss:

> The day I was made unemployed the bottom dropped out of my world. Being an activist in a factory, with my whole life structured and geared to the factory, and then suddenly, virtually overnight, to be divorced from all that, left me with a tremendous feeling of social isolation. That is one of the main effects of mass unemployment. [...] Who are the unemployed? As activists in the movement, we tend to overlook the importance of this question: the unemployed, in my experience, are not about to join the barricades, they are people with all sorts of problems. Many of them suffer from intense apathy, there are those at the bottom of despair. The unemployed are a broad spectrum of people.
>
> (*Marxism Today*, January 1984, p. 31)

In reading the testimony consider the following questions:

1. How does the account reflect on their experience of unemployment?
2. What does the qualitative testimony add to the regional statistics?
3. What other sources might reveal more about unemployment during these times?

that were present during this period of economic change (Griffin, 2023). Remembering these alternatives, such as the considerable work around the 1984-85 Miners' strike in Britain, is crucial for remembering place-based responses to these changes and the solidarity produced during those times.

The three examples introduced, of place writing, agricultural landscapes and deindustrialisation, begin to give some sense of the contrasting approaches to understanding place, as a more aggregated form of historical geography engagement. They reveal different approaches to understanding both rural and urban places. Whether through detailed place writing, engagements with labour histories, or closer engagement with personal memories and emotions, historical geographers have contributed widely to theorisations and empirical studies of place. The examples cited, though, also hint at the final scale of historical geography to be introduced here. They begin to indicate interrelations between place and connectivity, whether through migrant workers, the politics of solidarity or wider political economic forces and changes. As such, the final scale introduced here for working with historical geography, moves towards a more global sense of historical geography through a more sustained engagement with the geographies of connectivity.

GLOBAL HISTORICAL GEOGRAPHIES

The final section extends the prior engagements to reveal how connections might be uncovered through historical geography study. These have been implicit in the examples already given, the maritime worlds of ships are inherently international and cosmopolitan, yet here were framed as smaller spaces, whilst the relationship between migration, work and landscape, which are clearly informed by connections, was introduced as a way of understanding places. Here then, we switch our analysis towards a more explicitly relational sense of historical geography. We pay closer attention to the making of connections across scales, between places and through mobile lives. As in the previous sections, this is a subtle shift but marks a distinctive change of direction towards the global, international and mobilities, whereby we might attend to connections across scales. As such, historical geography might connect with contemporary reflections on globalisation, which can be defined as:

> The process whereby people, places, regions, and countries become more interlinked and more interdependent at a plane-tary scale. It also refers to the outcome of these processes.
>
> (Rogers, Castree and Kitchin, 2013, n.p.)

Doreen Massey's work is also pertinent here, situating place 'as articulated moments in networks of social relations and understandings, but where a larger proportion of those relations, experiences and understandings are constructed on a far larger scale' (Massey, 1991, p. 28). Her approach encourages geographers to think critically about the scalar language we might use and to attend to spatial relations in our approach to all spaces. Rather than viewing globalisation as simply forging new connections and spreading societal relations, she is keen to stress how such connections are experienced differently by different actors in different places. This troubles any notion of simply distinguishing between local and global.

For historical geographers this poses similarly important questions. David Featherstone (2008, p. 8) for example points out that work around globalisation and connectivity 'have been structured by a remorseless presentism' that position 'current forms of transnational political activity as a radical break with past forms of political practice.' In response, historical geographers have consistently challenged this ahistorical perspective to show how global connections have a much longer history, and how the perspective offered by globalisation might be reconsidered through past examples. The historical geographer sees great potential in revisiting the past through a spatial lens, attending to pasts with an eye for translocal and transnational relations. Three examples are raised below to illuminate this final scalar perspective. First, some engagements with the histories of migration are introduced through the perspective of Latvian women workers in Britain. Second, the chapter recognises how global relations are not always welcoming or accepting, through an engagement with racialised tensions. And finally, the chapter reflects on the use of global connections and imaginaries as informing solidarity practices, in particular through the historical geographies of anti-war movements. These are introduced as prompts to potentially shape your own thinking on more relational, global historical geographies.

Linda McDowell (2004) provides one such perspective through her engagements with Latvian women in post-Second World War Britain. These women arrived in Britain after the war and McDowell utilises oral history interviews to document their cultural memories, whilst also attending to the processes of forgetting. This close engagement with memory, particularly in relation to elements of displacement and refuge, begins to illustrate the complexities of engaging with memory (as is considered further in Chapter 3). Crucially, and in connection with the global framing provided here, such an approach begins to recognise the diversity of collective memory within a nation, for example, in this study, the little-known presence of Latvian women within Britain. Their stories, of arrival, displacement, violence and hope, are indicative of a perspective potentially hidden in the imagining of post-war Britain.

McDowell attends to these stories of Eastern Europe migration, primarily through seeking refuge rather than as economic migrants, illustrating more nuanced memories of conflict and displacement. She does so by paying particular attention to sensory memories:

> Food also played a role in fantasy and in memories of home, comforting young women in their journeys. As Laura explained:
>
> > We were in the train for 24 or more hours, with no food. And we girls, we were talking only about food, you know, how mum makes pancakes and this and that, you know. It helped us feel better.
>
> More exotic food features in Erna's memory of reaching safety and its associated luxuries:
>
> > When we arrived in the American zone and I remember, I remember seeing for the first time the white bread, it was white bread and oranges they were giving us.
>
> (McDowell, 2004, p. 716)

The associations uncovered here begin to reveal the powerful nature of memory that can recall in depth the detail of moments from the past. McDowell interviewed her participants over 50 years after some of the experiences of displacement, and the memories for some are particularly vivid. They are often quite troubling in nature as well as revealing some moments of collective solidarity, which persists. The research identifies how these memories are also attached to material objects and notes how the women would often recall some of the most violent elements of their journeys, from Latvia to Britain, through reference to a particular item, such as clothing. One woman described how 'she had been reluctant to wear yellow ever since that day as it brought back her feelings of helplessness and the long guilt she carried for being unable to prevent the other woman's rape' (McDowell, 2004, p. 715). These memories then combine the most violent experiences imaginable with the more mundane elements of domestic life and reveal something about how collective memory is forged, remembered and coped with. As we see through many examples within this book, the relationship between object and memory provides a methodological possibility for the historical geographer, in that objects might trigger particular memories and illicit further information about pasts.

An engagement with violence here leads us to a further troubling historical geography. McDowell indicates how displacement can be a violent process, particularly framed in relation to military conflict. The history of port towns and cities suggests that such processes of migration and mobility can be equally troubling on arrival and in life building within new places and spaces. Griffin and Martin (2021) provide one such insight through their study of the 'race riots' in Britain in 1919. They revisit these early twentieth century histories of violence to reveal a longer lasting history of racism as reflected through violence in British ports such as Glasgow, Liverpool, South Shields and Cardiff. Linking the violent events together begins to trouble any false sense of spontaneity relating to the violence and instead suggests how the response of a white working class towards foreign labour competition was largely informed by a connected force of white labourism (a solidarity amongst white workers which explicitly targeted workers of colour):

> A serious disturbance, which at moments amounted to riot, occurred yesterday afternoon at Broomielaw, Glasgow […] was the scene of furious fighting between white and coloured

sailors and firemen [...] A large and hostile crowd of British seamen and white sailors of other nationalities followed the coloured men to their lodging-house to which they ran for refuge.

Edinburgh Evening News, January 24, 1919

The analysis of an event like this is a challenging one. Newspaper reports like that above, reflect a complex dynamic between workers of different nationalities, in violent, racialised conflict. Griffin and Martin's analysis links together white trade union responses (with a particular focus on seafaring unions), as well as the economic conditions of unemployment and wage disparities, alongside the experiences of black sailor's wives and the wider communities associated with these events. In doing so, the authors are able to provide a more rounded version of the events which situates their making as well as considering their legacy (there is further racialised violence in the 1920s):

The combination of events and influences is presented to begin to disrupt distinctions between mundane and exceptional events and to consider the experiences within and beyond the riots of 1919. The 'race riots' were everyday encounters, with both instances linked to the process of signing on for work, that took on exceptional meaning, through rioting, but this dynamic was not spontaneous.

(Griffin and Martin, 2021, p. 6)

Crucially for this section, though, the events are little-known histories within British towns and cities which have a long history of migration, and in some instances racialised violence. The authors also stress how this violence is not the only story to tell, and that within these same places there are stories of inclusion and cohesion, and solidarity and resistance, contrasting these more exclusionary logics. What is clear from foregrounding these dynamics is the productive nature of a closer engagement with mobility and connections, as these were so integral to places like port towns which were in many ways defined by exchanged and migration, but equally potentially any place where Massey's relational sense of place can be extended to.

The sense of alternatives to more dominant narratives, and the possibilities for resistance, is carried forward into the final example for working with more global historical geographies. As indicated in Table 2.1, there are groups of historical geography scholarship that have strived to show the spatial politics of resistance and solidarity. These works have engaged closely with alternative acts of protest and organising, including those of workers, anti-colonialists and women, whilst also engaging with the potential for alternative world making which might move beyond the oppositional framing sometimes implied by the language of resistance. Much of this work has been driven by the recognition that organising practices are often stronger through their use of geography (e.g. solidarity movements) and that communities can become connected to campaigns beyond their immediate locality. These sentiments are pertinent for thinking with global historical geography and are briefly reflected upon with reference to anti-war movements.

During the First World War, there was notable opposition from campaigners and organisers who argued for peace and an end to the military conflict. This opposition was forged through varying positions, sometimes these were pacificist in nature whilst other campaigns centred upon a more political anti-war message (for example critiquing the profit making of munitions manufacturers). One place where these anti-war sentiments were particularly prominent was within Glasgow, Scotland. The diverse political reasons for opposition to the war were immediately apparent. At the end of 1915, there were anti-conscription rallies in Glasgow, political conferences to discuss positions on the war and broader practices of community organising throughout the city. A sense of international solidarity and a working class critique of war profit making, was central to these anti-war movements and this was further evident during a 'Peace Society platform' demonstration that passed the following resolution:

> That this meeting deplores the outbreak of War and declares it to be the outcome of Capitalism allied with Militarism, which has been consistently opposed by the organised workers and pacifists in all the countries concerned and this meeting sends

fraternal greetings to the working classes of and pacifists of Germany, Austria, Italy, Russia, France, Belgium, Servia, and all other countries.

(Forward, 15/8/14)

This spirit of internationalism, as documented in the newspapers of the political left, was prominent within Glasgow's oppositional groups to the war. One Glasgow based activist reflected this diversity in shaping anti-war sentiment. Helen Crawfurd channelled her anti-war efforts through the Women's Peace Crusade (WPC), as secretary, alongside other Glasgow based women (including Mary Barbour, Agnes Dollan and Ethel Kaye). Crawfurd had been heavily connected to suffragette campaigning prior to the war, and was a strong campaigner for women's rights before, during and after the war effort. The First World War marked a conflict within the suffragette movement, though, and Crawfurd decided to leave the movement due to their support for the war. Her political life was part of a network of likeminded communities, and her memoirs document how the global sharing of ideas and materials shaped her politics.

These women had a significant presence within the city, holding regular open-air meetings around Clydeside and producing leaflets, pamphlets and badges that were distributed throughout Scotland, and were shaped by a spirit of international solidarity. Reflecting on her involvement with this movement in her memoirs, Crawfurd stressed the importance of the street corner as a political meeting place during this period and these more unofficial meetings, when compared to the 'official' trade union forms of organising, were central to WPC organising. This anti-war sentiment was generally founded upon a spirit of international solidarity and was generally shaped through international networks, as evidenced by other Glasgow anti-war activists such as James Maxton and Guy Aldred. The efforts of campaigners like these begin to give a more practical sense of internationalism, as something which is practiced through campaigning and collective efforts to articulate solidarities. These efforts are generally grounded within places, such as Glasgow as raised here, but are not limited by place-based boundaries. Instead, they provide evidence of the active efforts of citizens to intervene in

BOX 2.3   Exercise – Working with global historical geographies

In more recent years, anti-war campaigns have again been visible in societies across the world. This was particularly noticeable in 2003 when millions of people campaigned against the war in Iraq. #iwasthere is available via https://www.wearemany.com/iwasthere/ and provides anonymous insights into the demonstrations that took place in over 60 countries on the 15th and 16th February 2003, involving over 6 million people. The accounts will provide an archive of experiences for future historians interested in this moment. Three perspectives from this collection are included below:

> I was one of several coach loads that travelled from Northampton to London that day. I had not felt that empowered since the anti-poll tax protests of the 1990's. The spirit and unity of that day will live with me forever. [London]
>
> Despite the freezing temperatures (-26 C), more than 150.000 peoples of all walks of life marched through the streets of Montreal downtown. Unions, Students, Women organisations, engaged Artists for Peace, teachers, Health workers, religious communities, Indigenous organisations, First Nations communities, immigrants, families... etc. all came together lead by the dynamic Anti-War movement in Quebec. [Montreal]
>
> Politicians didn't have the choice but to come and listen to this powerful message from citizens of Quebec and Canada. This great mobilization was possible first because of the deep-rooted history of pacifism in Quebec but also because of the hard work of mobilization during months ahead of the February 15 2003. [Montreal]

These are just three accounts from the millions of people who participated in the actions worldwide, but they being to reveal some of the geographies of solidarity found within the anti-war movement. Consider the following prompts in reading these extracts, and feel free to consult more at the weblink above:

1. In what ways do extracts above reflect a global historical moment?
2. In what ways might these experiences be considered on an individual basis? What are the individual motivations and imaginaries for participation?
3. What are the more collective organisations referred to here? How might the reflect wider networks of organising?

global geopolitical processes and military conflicts, revealing a more complex spatial politics between the local and the global.

The three examples above, plus the short exercise, begin to reveal the potential for relational understandings of historical geography, as forged through imaginary and material connections across, between and through places. The examples considered reveal more personal experiences of mobility, as well as place-based responses to migration and geopolitical conflict. As was implicit within the earlier scalar examples, the influence of global dynamics is found across our scalar devices. As such, it is often a question of emphasis when we come to research historical geographies and write our essays, projects and presentations. In concluding, the chapter reflects on the intersecting nature of the scales introduced. It does so to reveal the overlapping and complementary nature of the scales considered, and to encourage historical geographers to think carefully about their scale of engagement. This might allow you to find the geographies through your own historical interests (Figure 2.3).

Figure 2.3 Anti-war demonstrations – sites of historical geography, resistance and solidarity.

Source: Shutterstock: Sage Ross.

SUGGESTED READING

Three readings are selected below from the scales introduced above. Take time to consult these and consider the different ways in which historical geography research might be undertaken and written:

Micro historical geography:

McGeachan, C. (2018) '"A prison within a prison"? Examining the enfolding spatialities of care and control in the Barlinnie Special Unit', *Area*, 51(2), pp. 200–207.

Place based:

Emery, J. (2018) 'Belonging, memory and history in the north Nottinghamshire coalfield', *Journal of Historical Geography*, 59, pp. 77–89.

Global and connected historical geography:

McDowell, L. (2004) 'Cultural memory, gender and age: Young Latvian women's narrative memories of war-time Europe, 1944–1947', *Journal of Historical Geography*, 30, pp. 701–728.

CONCLUSIONS

This chapter has offered some contrasting perspectives for guiding the reader in their early engagements with historical geography. It started with some broader reflections upon disciplinary trends and approaches, whilst acknowledging some key theoretical works. These were then complemented with the three scalar approaches to introduce different approaches and writing of historical geographies. All three have stressed the geography of the past, albeit in quite contrasting ways. Micro-historical geographies highlighted the more intimate spaces of interactions, revealing how small spaces might indicate our most meaningful geographies and interactions, indicating how small spaces might also be considered as 'worlds.' Secondly, place-based histories were considered to indicate how historical geographers might engage with a sense of place through landscapes and sites, and their aggregated meaning through a widening of scale. Finally, the emphasis placed upon global historical geographies looked to stress mobility and connections through individuals, events and political practice. In these short summaries, the overlapping nature of the scalar enquiry might begin to emerge. The intimate can be found within the global, and indeed vice versa. The scalar approach adopted here has two primary aims. One as a means to present and understand contrasting approaches to research within historical geography, and two, as a means to continually stress the relational geographies through which the past might be understood.

As has been stressed throughout, these scales are not introduced as discrete modes of inquiry. Indeed, they overlap in many ways whereby the global informs the local, and connectivity is as likely to be encountered within smaller spaces such as those introduced through port spaces. The final example stresses this by encouraging a relational approach to the places and spaces considered. The anti-war demonstrations of 2003 were experienced by individuals in personal ways, within particular cities which felt their presence, whilst also being heavily connected to other sites.

An attentiveness to these geographical dynamics is a key contribution emergent from historical geography. This is expanded upon further in later chapters where the importance of theoretical perspectives and writing analytically is foregrounded. For now, though, the wide-ranging introductory chapters have sought to give a flavour of what might be possible through historical geography. The snippets from previous studies are intended to prompt further reading and engagement of your own. With these in mind, we now switch our attention to methodological reflections, by commenting in greater detail on how best to conduct historical geography research through engagement with the archive, memory, landscapes and objects.

REFERENCES

Awcock, H. (2021) 'Stickin' it to the man: The geographies of protest stickers', *Geography Compass*, 53(3), pp. 522–530.

Barcia, M. (2017) 'Going back home: Slave suicide in nineteenth-century Cuba', *Millars: Espai I Histria* 42(1), 49–73.

Boyle, J. (1977) *A sense of freedom*. London: Pan Books.

Emery, J. (2018) 'Belonging, memory and history in the north Nottinghamshire coalfield', *Journal of Historical Geography*, 59, pp. 77–89.

Featherstone, D. (2008) *Resistance, space and political identities: The makings of counter-global networks*. Chichester: Wiley-Blackwell.

Featherstone, D. (2012) *Solidarity: Hidden histories and geographies of internationalism*. London: Zed Books.

Ferretti, F. (2019) 'Rediscovering other geographical traditions', *Geography Compass*, 13(3), p. e12421.

Forsyth, I. (2012) *From dazzle to the desert: A cultural-historical geography of camouflage*. PhD thesis, University of Glasgow.

Foucault, M. (1965) *Madness and civilization: A history of insanity in the age of reason*. London: Tavistock.

Griffin, P. (2023) 'Unemployed workers' centres (1978–): Spatial politics, "non-movement", and the making of centres', *Antipode*, 55(2), pp. 393–414.

Griffin, P. and Martin, H. (2021) 'The 1919 "race riots" – Within and beyond exceptional moments in South Shields and Glasgow', *Political Geography*, 88, Article 102408.

Hasty, W. (2014) 'Metamorphosis afloat: Pirate ships, politics and process, c.1680–1730', *Mobilities*, 9(3), pp. 350–368.

Historic England (n.d.) The growth of the asylum – A parallel world. Available online: https://historicengland.org.uk/research/inclusive-heritage/disability-history/1832-1914/the-growth-of-the-asylum/. Last accessed: 8/11/2024

Lloyd, J. and Johnson, L. (2004) 'Dream stuff: The postwar home and the Australian Housewife, 1949-60', *Environment and Planning D: Society and Space*, 22, pp. 251–272.

Lorimer, H. (2019) 'Dear departed: Writing the lifeworlds of place', *Transactions of the Institute of British Geographers*, 44(2), pp. 331–345.

Magnusson, S.G. (no date) What is microhistory? [Online]. Available from: https://historynewsnetwork.org/article/23720. Last accessed: 8/4/2024

McDonagh, B. (2018) 'Feminist historical geographies: Doing and being', *Gender, Place & Culture*, 25(11), pp. 1563–1578.

McDowell, L. (2004) 'Cultural memory, gender and age: Young Latvian women's narrative memories of war-time Europe, 1944–1947', *Journal of Historical Geography*, 30, pp. 701–728.

McGeachan, C. (2018) '"A prison within a prison"? Examining the enfolding spatialities of care and control in the Barlinnie Special Unit', *Area*, 51(2), pp. 200–207.

Mitchell, D. (1996) *The lie of the land*. Minneapolis: University of Minnesota Press.

Moran, D. (2015) *Carceral geography: Spaces and practices of incarceration*. Farnham: Ashgate.

Naylor, S. (2005) 'Introduction: Historical geographies of science – places, contexts, cartographies', *The British Journal for the History of Science*, 38(1), pp. 1–12.

Philo, C. (1987) '"Fit localities for an asylum": The historical geography of the nineteenth century "mad-business" in England as viewed through the pages of the Asylum Journal', *Journal of Historical Geography*, 13(4), pp. 398–415.

Radcliffe, S. (2017) 'Decolonising geographical knowledges', *Transactions of the Institute of British Geography*, 42(3), pp. 329–333.

Rediker, M. (2004) *Villains of all nations: Atlantic pirates in the golden age*. London: Verso.

Rediker, M. (2007) *The slave ship: A human history*. London: John Murray.

Rogers, A., Castree, N. and Kitchin, R. (2013) 'Place', in *A dictionary of human geography*. Oxford University Press. Retrieved 5 Feb. 2025, from https://www.oxfordreference.com/view/10.1093/acref/9780199599868.001.0001/acref-9780199599868-e-1399

Williamson, B. (2023) 'Historical geographies of place naming: Colonial practices and beyond', *Geography Compass*, 17(5), p. e12687.

Zavala Guillen, A.L. (2023). 'Women in the Geographies of Marronage – Territorial intimacy as a freedom strategy: The Case of María de Los Santos and Her Bonga.' *Fronteras de la Historia*, 28(2), 76–99.

3

ARCHIVES AND PRACTISING HISTORICAL GEOGRAPHY

INTRODUCTION

As we have seen in the previous two chapters, historical geography exists as a body of work and ideas that demonstrate different knowledges of the world and its people in all kinds of interesting variations. They operate on varying scales and are attentive to different theoretical positions and subject areas, highlighting the diversity of the sub-discipline. However, importantly for our discussions into researching historical geography it must be noted that historical geography is also a *practice,* and a great deal of attention is now being placed on exploring, understanding and critiquing the processes involved in 'doing' historical geography research.

In many ways it can feel quite daunting to start historical research. Questions surface regarding where do I begin and what do I need to do to get started? We will cover the more practical nature of these questions in Chapter 5 however this chapter seeks to introduce you to debates within historical geography regarding archives and archival practice. It allows you to view and consider how the archive has become such an important and critical place for excavations of the past and is a contentious and evolving site of historical geography scholarship. For many the archive remains a mysterious entity, and you may never have been to or thought about archives before. Don't worry, this is not unusual! However, in your journey into historical geography research it becomes an important site of encounter and one that requires you to know and understand a wider set of conversations relating to how we find and use sources from the past. This chapter is an attempt to introduce you to such debates, allowing you

DOI: 10.4324/9781003483588-3

to gain an understanding of the archive and how these fit with the wider development of your research. It is an attempt to familiarise you with the archive and archival research, developing your awareness and confidence with exploring the archive for yourself.

This chapter will begin by engaging with the archive and the place of archival research in historical geography. We will concentrate on different ways of working *with* archives and how this can lead us to considering places and voices in alternative formations. Discussions will centre on thinking through gaps and silences, leading us to explore the ways in which historical geographers have developed and undertaken practices that lead to a wider exploration of the margins of history and their geographies. The chapter will end by reflecting on a widening of the archive in historical geography to encompass landscapes, material matter and digital realms, discussing the ongoing implications for practice and research.

METHODS, METHODOLOGY AND A TURN TO CONSIDERING PRACTICE

Since Hayden Lorimer (2009), in his essay discussing archives and fieldwork, reemphasised the lack of attention in historical geography to talking in depth about methods and practice, there has been a wealth of new insights into the different ways that historical geographers *do* their research. Debates relating to the lack of methodological discussion within the sub-field had been echoed by Robert Mayhew (2007) where he reflected on the lack of sustained critical engagement with methods within historical geography, signalling to the absence of discussion since Alan Baker's and Mark Billinge's *Period and Place* (1982). Lorimer and Mayhew's insights offered important reflections into the ways that historical research was often deemed to be an intuitive process that required a lack of methodological explanation or critical reflection, something that was simply 'done' by the researcher and remained largely unspoken. This is evident in earlier work in historical geography that whilst rich in empirical depth and detail, left little space for discussing how the research was undertaken and the effects of these practices on the research itself. It is also evident in earlier methods textbooks which often dedicated little space to considering the practices of archival research in critical ways, conveying a mostly instrumental approach to undertaking and interpreting the work. Attention was frequently placed on considering aspects of working with sources and concerning evidence, which remain important aspects of historical geography research that we discuss in Chapter 5 yet increasingly calls to more widely speak about 'method' have greatly shaped aspects of practice in the sub-discipline.

The critical turn in human geography, in conjunction with the rise of post-structuralist and post-modernist thinking in the wider social sciences and humanities, led to a greater emphasis being placed on *how* research was conducted. This provided important fertile ground within historical geography for the development of discussions relating to practice, with a number of methods textbooks, edited collections and researcher events centring around sharing and developing aspects of practice and 'doing' historical geograph*ies* (see https://hgrg.org.uk/). Drawing from rich theoretical terrains and varied philosophical approaches as highlighted further in Chapter 4, plurality and multiplicity gained importance with researchers noting the variety and complexities of places and practices associated with undertaking historical work, placing it in context with wider methodological discussions within the discipline.

Key to these evolving debates regarding practice, is the role of the archive and archival research in doing historical geography work. A central aspect to historical geography is its embedded interest in the (changing) geography of the past and therefore the modes of accessing these past worlds, lives and places remains deeply connected to the archive and the sources it contains. As Alan Baker (1997), in his seminal piece 'The dead don't answer questionnaires' conveys, the focus on the past can have a constraining effect on 'doing' historical geography placing a stronghold on utilising archives and deploying archival methods. Yet, as we will see in the following sections, these restricted terrains are shifting as historical geographers begin to see archives in new ways and generate new practices of working with and beyond the archive in their studies.

ARCHIVES

When we think of an archive, we often conjure images of large institutional places, such as libraries and record offices. Our minds may take us to dark, dusty and quiet places where important documents of the past are wheeled out to us on squeaky trolleys and touched only through white-gloved hands. Many popular perceptions of archival work are given to us through film and television with many archivists showing frustration at the *Who do you think you are?* effect that portrays very little about the realities of archival practice and the labour associated with undertaking archival work. This popularisation of archives as institutionally placed remains an important aspect of archival research for many, however, it is also important to expand this thinking to consider the various places where materials from the past can be deposited, stored and accessed. This can include more personal collections, held in homes, gardens or attics, material remnants evident on buildings and landscapes and digital traces held in phones and visible on social media platforms to name but a few. Whilst these places may not identify themselves with the term archive and store their information in very different ways, thinking about them as archives can be a revealing and rewarding enterprise in historical geography research. In expanding our thinking of what and where an archive can be, we diversify the materials that can be considered as archival sources to be worked with in our research.

Archives exist in multiple forms, but they are always places where the production of knowledge occurs. Yet this is a complex process and is tied up in a range of social, cultural, political and emotional relations. For Miles Ogborn (2011, p. 88) the archive 'is a place of memory and a place of loss. It is a place of power and a place of weakness. It is a place of excitement and a place of tedium,' signalling to the complex and contradictory nature of such places for making knowledge. In many ways archives can be thought of as very different *kinds of places* for geographical interrogation and insight. Ogborn (2011) reveals that in one sense the archive is 'a venue for the localisation of knowledge' becoming a place where original material remnants of the past such as maps, instruments, photographs, manuscripts and many others are stored and held. Yet they are also places where people wishing to produce certain validated knowledge of the past must go through in order to reproduce these original remnants of knowledge in other forms (Ogborn, 2011). In many ways this simply demonstrates the importance of the archive as both a container and a vessel of knowledge production. In centring the archive as a special kind of place, Ogborn is drawing attention to

Figure 3.1 Royal Geographical Society Archives – the Foyle Reading room.
Source: © Royal Geographical Society (with IBG).

the fluxes and flows of people, objects and knowledges that are continually in operation throughout our encounters with the archive. This set of encounters highlights it distinctive qualities, yet it also initiates a diverse set of relational complexities that makes thinking about the archive a less-than-straightforward process.

Figures 3.1 and 3.2 step inside an archive of disciplinary relevance. They are included on behalf of the Royal Geographical Society and show both the reading room (a space where archival materials are consulted) and the shelving units (the space where archival materials are stored and maintained). Scholars have utilised these archives to study the history of our discipline and to consider the role of geography in society. The inclusion of these images here, though, is primarily to illustrate the archive as a space where research is conducted. The nature of this research necessitates interactions between researcher and archivist as well as researcher and material. As noted above, archival spaces differ in size, space and style but the nature of the research is often similar. Archival research requires considerable time spent within these spaces and needs close examination of archival material.

Figure 3.2 Royal Geographical Society Archives – shelving and archival stores.
Source: © Royal Geographical Society (with IBG).

ARCHIVAL MATERIALS

As described above, the diversity of types and forms of archives leads to a multiplicity in the kinds of materials that can be found within them. In Chapter 5 we will explore in more detail different ways of working with varying types of historical materials however it is important to stress at this stage that we need an awareness of the different materials that we may encounter in archives and the ways that this structures and inhibits our research. Whilst there are too many types of sources to consider in one chapter there is merit in showcasing some selected examples to highlight the scale of the variety evident in historical geography research and the questions this raises for the doing of historical geography. The following examples demonstrate a handful of ways in which historical geographers have utilised different archival sources to tell the histories of the discipline and the development of geographical knowledge, opening up questions for considering our choice of sources and what they both offer, constrain and distort in the doing of our research.

Maps are often considered to be a key data source in historical geography, again in line with the popular conception of what geography is associated to be in our wider imaginings. Recently there has been a reawakening of interest in working with maps represented as models to explore further the nature of cartographic practice and display. Mike Heffernan and Benjamin Thorpe (2018), for example, use the Morrison-Bell's Tariff Wall Map to consider the entangled histories of cartography, economics and geo-politics in early twentieth-century Britain. Clive Morrison-Bell (1871–1956) was a British Member of Parliament who made use of maps and cartographic models in political campaigns before and after the First World War, and the authors focus on one of his most famous creations, the Tariff Wall Map (TWM). The map was a three-dimensional cartographic model of Europe, on which international borders were represented by the inclusion of physical walls. The authors argue that focussing on the TWM offers important insight into the political uses and abuses of cartography, portraying new ways of knowing and exploring the histories of geography as they are invoked and performed in different spaces of power. However, whilst the map itself sits as the catalyst for the study's investigation the authors note their use of a wider set of sources to inform their investigations. Heffernan and Thorpe (2018) share that they use a wide set of sources relating to the Morrison-Bell's papers held in the Parliamentary Archives in London, including newspaper cuttings, diaries, newspaper articles, correspondence and an unpublished autobiography. In utilising a combination of sources, the authors are able to unravel some of the complex geographies associated with the TWM's making and circulation, delving further into what this model means and conveys. This combination of sources, across varying archives, leads to both a wider contextualisation of the TWM and a more in-depth understanding of its making, offering new and innovative insights into the histories of cartographic practice.

In her seminal excavation of the historiographies of women in British geography through a focus on the geographical work of women from 1850 to 1970, Avril Maddrell (2009) utilises a diversity of methods and sources to address a significant gap in the histories of the discipline. When discussing her archival practice Maddrell turns to Anne Burton's (2005, p. 8) reflections on process:

> ... history is not merely a project of fact retrieval ... but also a set of complex processes of selection, interpretation, and even creative invention − processes set in motion by, among other things, one's personal encounter with the archive, the history of the archive itself, and the pressure of the contemporary moment on one's reading of what is to be found there.

Maddrell's awareness of the distortions and gaps associated with her archival work leads her to utilise the archive as an 'opportunity' to engage with the lives of these women and their biographies. One type of source that is significant to Maddrell's work is that of the obituary. Obituaries are a form of textual memorial often produced in newspapers and academic journals, that offer partial and compacted biographies of individuals and their lives. In her investigations into women geographers, Maddrell notes the need to be critically aware of the limitations of the type of source and her own uses of them. For example, obituaries are often celebratory in style, yet Maddrell draws attention to the art of reading between the lines of certain words and phrases to illuminate more complex subject positions. Maddrell highlights that certain women geographers are described in these sources as 'formidable,' 'determined' and 'difficult' signalling to the underlying themes about women that can be read through these types of sources. Throughout her work information from obituaries are used alongside other archival sources and oral histories, to provide and supplement dates and context to the women's lives, relationships and careers, also at times providing photographs and visual representations of these women. They provide an important way in which to understanding aspects of the lives and careers of certain women geographers. However, as Maddrell argues the absence of an obituary is also highly significant in historical research, signalling to the potential erasure of these lives and work from the discipline.

Innes Keighren's (2007) curiosity regarding the fragmentary everyday sources that appear in archives draw us to consider the importance of quotidian events to the researching and writing of the histories of geography. In researching the papers of eminent geomorphologist William Morris Davis within the Association of American Geographers archives, a mundane detail about Davis's everyday life caught his eye: 'two shredded wheat biscuits and a half pint of milk and salt. No sugar, thank you; too obesifying' (Keighren, 2007, p. 47). The source of this seemingly trivial detail came through an undated letter written by Davis and retained in Box 156 of the archive marked External Relations. Keighren notes that his attention to Davis's voicing of his favourite breakfast cereal led him to wonder about the 'clutter' that the archives of our lives can contain. The history of geography has often been written utilising official documents of professional practice taking pride of place in archival collections. However, Keighren ponders what would happen if historical geographers allowed themselves to rummage in these more mundane records of a life and write the histories of geography from these more personal remains. This set of provocations regarding the seemingly mundane or everyday aspects of individuals lives provide new ways of considering sources, suggesting challenges to what has conventionally been seen to matter in historical geographical research.

Whilst these examples do not cover the depth and variety of sources that are engaged with across all areas of historical geography, they highlight some of the contours of working with varied sources to explore different aspects of a topic, in this case the history of geography. Table 3.1 showcases further some examples of the sources used

Table 3.1 Selected examples of sources used in historical geography research.

Source	Research Area
School Log Books	Histories of Weather (Naylor et al., 2022)
Protest Stickers	Land and Resistance (Awcock, 2021)
Eggs	Nature and Science (Cole, 2016)
Monuments	Inequalities (Legg, 2025)
Travel Albums	Exploration (Felix Driver, 2000)
Guidebooks	Mobilities (Ferriday, 2023)
Photographs	Colonialism (Gough, 2023)
Dissertations	History of Geography (Bruinsma, 2021)
Guitars	Labour (Gibson and Warren, 2023)
Feathers	Craft and Crafting (Patchett, 2017)
Journals	Geography Education (Norcup, 2015)

in historical geography and their associated research areas to help support your thinking in these areas. The examples in the table illuminate the diversity of sources that can be utilised within historical geography research but also lead us to consider the widening of the archive that they reveal. Whilst historical texts, photographs and guidebooks may feel familiar to our conceptions of what is likely to be held within the archive, eggs, protest stickers and feathers may feel less so. These examples highlight the validity of both utilising more conventional and more unusual sources in our research of the past. Expanding our engagement with sources can lead to new explorations of key geographical issues such as labour and colonialism and can also take our work into new creative dimensions such as the world of craft and resistance movements.

When considering our practice as historical geographers undertaking archival research it becomes vital to consider the histories and geographies of the places themselves. This is because what we are engaging with and interpreting from the archive is intimately bound to these wider historical geographies of place and knowledge production. As noted earlier in the chapter, moving away from considering the archive as purely a source of information and material evidence, to thinking about it as a place itself develops its exploratory potential and moves us to consider more clearly the power relations that underpin the practices of archival work.

The historical geography (or geographies) of the archive is intimately bound to the histories of state formation and is therefore connected to the rise of a particular form of archive; that of the public archive. In many ways the public archive is the version of archives that is ingrained in popular imagination as described previously and exists today as an emblem of a traditional archival space. A number of historical geographers have examined state power within this context and have considered the formation of the public archive as a colonial and imperial historical geography. We have already touched upon this in Chapter 1 with reference to 'operation legacy' and the controversy surrounding the records relating to colonial and postcolonial Kenya.

Related research has demonstrated the ways in which different information was created, stored and recovered, then worked through across a series of important imperial geographies, including colonies, trading stations and the processes of ongoing imperial warfare. This work therefore highlights how these geographies have important consequences for the archives themselves and the knowledge that is therefore produced through them. For example, it has shaped the very nature of the archive itself, what the building looks like, what they contain, who worked there and who has permission to access the space. It also shapes the content of the archive, with certain materials being given different weight and positions. As Jim Duncan (1999) in his work on complicity and resistance in the colonial archive demonstrates, documents that were important to those in colonial power, such as legal or administrative pieces, were kept in manuscript form leading to an assertion of power through the archive by the state. In many ways unravelling the colonial and imperial historical geographies of archives reinforces the notion that archives are, and always has been, places of competing interests laden with complex power relations.

Considering these ideas through grounded empirical studies has allowed a multitude of historical geographers to consider the site of the archive in relation to imperial and colonial legacies. Drawing significantly on postcolonial and feminist frameworks for considering the reconstitution of knowledge, these studies emphasise the complex ways in which historical geographers attempt to make sense of their own use of these collections, assessing their positionalities and concerns for potential complicity with colonialist practices of power/knowledge (Duncan, 1999). We will now consider an example of work that helps us to explore the move more widely considered as a turn in the social sciences from archive-as-source to archive-as-subject(Withers, 2002).

Ruth Craggs (2008), for example, explores the Library of the Royal Empire Society (RES) from its foundation in 1868 to the mid-twentieth century. Throughout her article the RES is described as both an Archive and Library, highlighting the slippery nature of the terms and the difficulties of denoting specific collections in certain ways. Craggs plots a brief history of the RES noting its foundations as the Colonial Society in 1868, and appearing as a learned society where members were drawn from those with an interest in Empire. Craggs highlights the changes to the RES, both in terms of its name and management structures, but also in terms of its architecture and geography with the library being redeveloped across its histories for a variety of practical and political reasons. Craggs's insights foreground the importance of the practices of the library staff and the physical structure itself for (re)creating and (re)enforcing the imaginative geographies of Empire:

> The physical layout also acted to unite the territories under a certain theoretical idea. The Inner Library provided a central point from which the rest of the collection should be understood, as Prue Scarlett, who worked at the RES from 1962 to 1997 explained:'If you imagine a core and then all the bits coming off it, which were the individual countries, but the individual countries were linked back to and understood through the core'. The Inner Library held general material describing the theoretical base of Empire, the linking thread which connected the diverse territories in the main body of the Library.Thus the collection was organised in the same way that Empire itself was imagined; it contained a central core where ideas were produced and which acted to unite the diverse peripheral sections.
>
> (Craggs, 2008, p. 57)

For Craggs, in order to understand the different ways in which knowledges in such places as the RES Library produces imaginative geographies, attention must not only centre on the archival materials themselves but on the wider set of people, their visions, practices and spaces. Attention to these spaces micro-geographies and individual topographies, including the mundane everyday practices of libraries and their staff which includes such practices as classifying, collecting, ordering and display and their technologies provides important access into the types of knowledges produced. This also points towards the importance of funding and resources for these archives, as well as the labour required within these settings (Griffin, 2018). This is something to be mindful of when researchers consider how they access the past, highlighting the many ways through which archives are made.

WORKING WITH ARCHIVES

What becomes visible in our reflections upon the archive and archival practice, so far, are that issues of power are crucial to the production and reproduction of geographical knowledges. As we have seen in our discussions, issues of power are deeply related to the people and practices associated with shaping archives, and this can be demonstrated through thinking about the foundations of the very notion of an archive. Derrida and Prenowitz (1995, pp. 9–10) relay this in their discussions of the meanings of the term archive and the ways in which this intersects with issues of power:

> As is the case for the Latin *archivum* or *archium* (a word that is used in the singular, as was the French "*archive*," formerly employed as a masculine singular: "*un archive*"), the meaning of "archive," its only meaning, comes to it from the Greek *arkheion*: initially a house, a domicile, an address, the residence of the superior magistrates, the *archons*, those who commanded. The citizens who thus held and signified political power were considered to possess the right to make or to represent the law. On account of their publicly recognized authority, it is at their home, in that *place* which is their house (private house, family house, or employee's house), that official documents are filed. The archons are first of all the documents' guardians. They do not only ensure the physical security of what is deposited and of the substrate. They are also accorded the hermeneutic right and competence. They have the power to interpret the archives.

These arguments reassert the significance of thinking about the archive as a particular type of place and draw to attention the ways in which power and archives connect in terms of access, ownership, and what gets kept and stored, and equally what is destroyed. For Derrida and Prenowitz (1995) the archive can act as a symbol to represent the current power being exercised in a particular time and place. Growing debates relating to the silencing and erasure of histories of Indigenous and First Nation Peoples through the restrictive nature of archival access and collection, conveys the current consequences of powerful state actors controlling memory and representation through the archive. In your own research, it might be that you want to trace a particularly marginalised perspective and that their voice might not be reached because of such power relations of the archive, something which Saidiya Hartman (2008) has described in her engagements with the archives of transatlantic slavery where the traces of women slaves are only found in records of their slave names and through their slave owners.

A range of theorists have explored dimensions of power in relation to the archive giving insight into the differing ways in which aspects of power infiltrate our 'doing' of historical geography. Processes of order and classification have received a great deal of theoretical attention. Drawing on French theorist Bruno Latour's arguments relating to the structuring of information through classification systems and processes of ordering, Miles Ogborn stresses the prominence of thinking critically and carefully about the role of order in the archive:

> Order is the key. It is the key to remembering the past, distant or recent, in order to have some purchase on it. It is the key to using the archive to bring the past back for the benefit of those in the present and the future. But different orders may produce different accounts of the past.
>
> (Ogborn, 2011, p. 89)

This is further reflected upon by Michel Foucault in his work *The Order of Things* (2001) where he discusses what he terms as the 'archaeological method.' For Foucault, archaeology is 'an enquiry whose aim is to rediscover [...] within what space of order knowledge is constituted [and is a] description of the archive' (2001, p. 57). It is a form of discourse analysis concerned with discursive practices – who is speaking, when, where, and what authority, etc. – paying close attention to the connections between knowledge and location, and how discursive practices are shaped by material conditions and relations of power and government. These complex processes have spatial resonances as described by Chris Philo (1992) who draws to attention Foucault's alertness to 'spaces of dispersion' and 'archaeological' approach to history demonstrating the importance of geography to considering notions of archival order. Maintaining order and creating organising principles are key factors in the creation and maintenance of the archive for it gives the archive and their systems an evidentiary quality, allowing them to be used and understood through certain frameworks. This might manifest in the forms of cataloguing and recording of material which might in turn shape how we then search and encounter the archive. This therefore brings to the fore a wealth of critical questions regarding our use of ordering systems which is particularly pertinent in studies relating to colonial archives (Clayton, 2021).

Recent historical geography work into digital archives and the processes of digitisation reveals some of the complex power relations associated with ordering and access (Hodder and Beckingham, 2022). Whilst not exclusively the domain of digital archives, the processes involved in accessing and navigating these archives move beyond the traditional systems of the 'analogue' archive. Hodder and Beckingham in their discussions of recombinant historical geographies draw to attention the complex relations that exist between order, classification and power when using digital archives, and the dangers that exist in not considering these in our work:

> Power in the digital archive appears to move from the archivist to the researcher. After all, online we arrive at materials not through the arrangement of the archive, but through tools that prioritise *our* search terms. This is the 'efficiency' and 'empowerment' promised by all digital platforms: the ability to surgically extract only those sources that speak directly to our research questions. But it is also the illusion of digital archives: it is not the researcher who is creating these new connections. The language of end-user empowerment masks the fact that it is the

platform that delivers recombination – not us. The shift of power in digital archives is not from archivists to researchers, but from archivists to algorithms.

(2022, p. 1302)

It is clear that similarly to other forms of archives there is great benefit to embracing and engaging with the range of tools that enable us to engage with archival systems however it is important to not make assumptions about the illusion of 'neutrality' of online digital platforms in our search for historical materials. As Hodder and Beckingham (2022) stress power does not dissipate with the rise of digital archives it simply shifts, and it is important to stay attentive to the new ways in which our research with the past is being affected by (often invisible) systems of order and classification.

BOX 3.1 Exercise – Archives and order

Reflecting upon order and classification in the archive and how this connects to issues of power can be very helpful for considering our own use of archive systems and the subsequent knowledges it produces.

Consider the example of Digital Panopticon: https://www.digitalpanopticon.org/

Imagine you are undertaking a historical geography research project into carceral spaces. You are interested in researching penal outcomes for female prisoners in Britain between 1850 and 1890.

Consider how you would begin to use this database to find relevant archival materials:

- What terms would you use to search for materials?
- What sources does your search compile?
- How relevant are these sources for your project?
- How many sources would you use from your search?
- What is missing or problematic about this process of searching?

It is often useful to document your process of searching and analysing archives (whether virtual or in-person) in this way as this can inform your writing of a methodology and your description of your research practice.

EMOTIONS AND THE ARCHIVAL ENCOUNTER

Recent attention to considering the archival encounter in historical geography research and wider engagements with the archive in the social sciences and humanities, have given rise to a number of questions relating to power and control in the archive. Thinking about the archival encounter illuminates the range of stories that exist about the type of places archives are imagined to be, in relation to past, present and future engagements, and the often-jarring actualities of the encounter in practice. One particularly notable account of such an archival story comes from Jacques Derrida, who developed his earlier work above into the now famous book called *Archive Fever* (1996). The groundings of this work are complex, centring on a deconstructive analysis of the notion of archiving. However, it usefully brings to light aspects of the archival encounter that are thought-provoking and compelling. For example, in comparing the archival search with our own human search for an origin, Derrida describes the feverish search as 'mal d'archive':

> It is to burn with a passion. It is never to rest, interminably, from searching for the archive, right where it slips away. It is to run after the archive, even if there's too much of it, right where something in it an archives itself. It is to have a compulsive, repetitive, and nostalgic desire for the archive, an irrepressible desire to return to the origin, a homesickness, a nostalgia for the return to the most archaic place of absolute commencement.
>
> (Derrida, 1996, p. 71)

For many writing about the archival encounter an inevitable feeling of dissatisfaction and frustration for what is there and what is not, shines through. What can be found and what remains missing become key drivers of the 'mal d'archive' setting in motion an insatiable voyage that can never have a discernible end. Many historical geographers have become captivated by the processes and practices of working with what remains, turning to consider different frameworks, such as the trace, to reflect more deeply on how to work in these difficult archival terrains (McGeachan, 2016).

The rise of interest in considering the human stories of research with (and within) archives has led to a stronger consideration of the embodied and emotional terrains of historical research. This aligns with a stronger emphasis throughout the discipline relating to emotional geographies and their importance in varied elements of research. Cultural historian Carolyn Steedman follows in Derrida's, and others, view, and provides a critical account of Derrida's notion of 'archive fever' at the beginning of her captivating book *Dust* (2001). For Steedman, the accounts of working with historical materials have important stories to tell about the archive and these themselves, she argues, are the 'stuff' of historical scholarship. In *Dust* she accounts her own experience of archive fever:

> Actually, quite apart from anything written by Derrida, or anything reflected by his critics, Archive Fever comes on at night, long after the archive has shut for the day ... For the fever – the feverlet, the precursor fever – usually starts at the end of the penultimate day in the record office. Either you must leave tomorrow (train times, journeys planned, a life elsewhere) or the record office will shut for the weekend ... You know *you will not finish*, that there will be something left unread, unnoted, untranscribed ....
>
> (Steedman, 2001, pp. 17–18)

Steedman talks in detail about the worries and concerns that haunt her waking (and sometimes sleeping) thoughts on the archival work she is undertaking; the pain of sitting for long periods of time looking over documents, the expense of time and travelling to and from archives, the fear of not being able to locate the documents required, etc., all conveying the embodied and personal challenges of archival work. These stories of the archive bring to the fore the importance of considering the embodied encounter of archival practice but also the turn towards self-reflection about the practice of doing archival work and the influence this has on the versions of histories produced. The loneliness, distress but also the joys and pleasures of doing such research have an impact on the ways in which we engage with historical materials and subsequently how we write about them. They matter.

In this regard, historical geography is not that far removed from more contemporary research in that the work can be challenging and the research can stay with you. Equally, there is scope for many helpful collaborations to emerge through conducting the research. One way in which historical geographers have conveyed this mattering is in relation to care. Trevor Wideman (2023) shares ethnographic experiences from their own archival encounters to highlight the relational aspects to care that can be present in archival research. Reflecting upon their experiences as a PhD researcher in a Canadian planning archive, Wideman highlights receiving care in the space:

> In one of my cities of interest, this was a difficult task. The archive was underfunded and housed in a bare-bones space, and some materials were difficult to find, as they were either uncatalogued or unavailable in online searches, a common problem for some archives (see Sahadeo 2005). Upon entering this archive, I was lost. I knew that there was a lot of material there but was unsure of how to search for it. After some extended conversations with the reference archivists on duty, they were able to provide me with access to several spreadsheets with lists that circulated internally but were not made available online. These spreadsheets led me to valuable resources. Further, on hearing my research topic, a different archivist appeared with some urban planning materials which they had just entered into their database. The materials in those folders, unknown to me at the time, would form the basis for a dissertation chapter and a peer reviewed journal article.
>
> (2023, p. 400)

For Wideman this sense of relational care shown to them by the archivist enabled a more productive and rewarding archival encounter that signified the importance of building relationships within archival research. For many archival institutions, particularly but not exclusively community-led archives, a lack of funding and resourcing can lead to challenges for the researcher to locate, access and work with the archival materials held. As Wideman highlights the importance of building relationships and respecting the skills, expertise and time of archivists and volunteers working in archives is crucial for generating caring research practice that transcends some of the hierarchical power relations embedded in archives and research.

GAPS AND SILENCES IN ARCHIVES

Greater attention to the multiple embodied and emotional stories of archival encounters and thinking of the archive-as-subject has led to a deeper consideration of archival *practice*. As previously discussed, what the archive holds and what it does not, the ways in which it is organised and items found, and our own personal orientations towards it, all shapes the stories told in our research. However, what gets written about from and through the archive differs over time and space and is connected to the changing ideas about knowledge and knowledge production. Whilst a great deal of attention often centres on what the archive holds, increased interest into what is missing or hidden from the archive has led to historical geographers questioning absences in the archive. This focus on absence (sometimes described as silences and gaps) is not, however, always detrimental to historical research. In fact, it can drive and inspire new ways of considering the past and the practices associated in its reconstruction. It can even become an object of study in and of itself. For example, Felix Driver and Lowri Jones explore the hidden histories of exploration through attention to the roles of locals and intermediaries illuminating new perspectives on the practices of exploration and the knowledges that were produced (https://www.rgs.org/our-collections/stories-from-our-collections/online-exhibitions/hidden-histories-of-exploration). Therefore, the search for new critical and intricate ways of telling historical geographies has led to an increased interest in absence, gaps and silences, with many historical geographers actively working on what cannot be found in archives.

Caroline Bressey's (2002) work highlights a number of ways in which working with absence and gaps in the archive can inspire and generate new ways of understanding and hearing marginalised and ignored histories. Using the Barnardo's Victorian archive, Bressey works through the gaps to uncover the historical geography of black women who found themselves in children's homes, asylums, prisons and on the stage. For Bressey (2002, p. 354) 'accessing the history of visible minorities, particularly that of women, requires more imaginative ways of researching' and she turns to the use of photographic archives as a key resource for her work. Through engaging with Barnardo's archives through the lens of race, Bressey is able to draw out case studies that highlight some of the experiences of black women and children and to showcase the presence of these lives in Victorian Britain.

The turn towards thinking about absence relates theoretically to issues discussed in this chapter, particularly connecting to considering 'other' voices, places and experiences than traditional historical accounts. These frameworks have led to an increased attempt to create and tune into new ways of 'doing' historical research and working with archival sources. To work through the gaps, silences and cracks of history many researchers have turned to techniques such as 'reading against' or 'reading along' the archival grain. For Sarah de Leeuw (2012) reading against the archival grain gives researchers the opportunity to think less about the contents of the archival materials themselves and instead to be more attuned to the wider systems of power that have (re)produced and legitimised these knowledges. Drawing on the historian Ann Stoler's (2009) work on the political and affective forms of archival production a number of historical geographers have turned to reading 'along the archival grain' to pay critical attention to the archival materials and an emotive orientation to the physical space of the archive, their stories, and the documents they hold. The contrasts between these archival practices are described by de Leeuw as:

> The difference between working 'along' as opposed to 'with' the archival grain is that, unlike the latter's connotation of passively accepting the archival record, the former requires a committed, impassioned and emotive response to the archival record, a recognition of what Ann Laura Stoler calls the 'the pulse of the archive'.
>
> (2012, p. 275)

For many historical geographers utilising these methods they seeking to question and contest systems of power offering opportunities to see emergent moments of resistance and autonomy. In simpler terms, these principles call for more critical engagements with archival materials and ask us to question how the material we are confronted with was produced, for what purpose was it created and what audiences it was intended for. We might also begin to consider the voice and tone of the material, as well as the absences and exclusions. Rather than simply reproducing the past as we find it, instead we might begin to read the material more critically, utilising skills and approaches more akin to textual or discourse analysis.

BOX 3.2 Exercise – Exploring personal archives

As we have identified thinking about archives as different kinds of places for knowledge production can be a challenging endeavour and centring in on our own personal archives can be a good place to begin to consider some of these thoughts and complexities in miniature.

Start by selecting an item that you own that you feel is part of your 'personal archive'

Perhaps this is something you have kept that is meaningful to you in some way or something that has been handed down to you through family or friendships. Think about how easy it is to find something to work with. Are you someone who keeps items from your past or someone who chooses to pass on or destroy these traces of your past life and connections?

Move to thinking further about the location of your item

Where do you keep this item? Is it easily accessible? Have you locked this away or can anyone see this?

Now consider the item itself and begin to explore its form and/ or function?

Is this a physical item that can be handled or does it exist only in the virtual realm? Is it textual, visual or material in nature? Is it something that is known and identifiable to others or distinctive only to you? Does the item stand alone or does it sit in connection with other items in your archive? Is it fragile or robust?

Turn your engagement to what information the item contains

What does the item tell you about and how does it show this? Does it contain a lot of information or a little? What kind of information does it convey? Does this information make sense to you or are there parts that feel difficult to understand?

Now turn your attention to your own practice of working with the item

How did you feel interpretating the item? Were you confident or unsure? Did your position as being the owner of the archive change your interpretation of the information from the item?

Finally, imagine giving your item to someone else to work with

How does it feel thinking of your item being engaged with and interpreted by another? What do you feel they might need to understand about your item? How would you like them to work with your item? Is there anything you would feel uncomfortable with others doing with this item?

These steps help us to think about the nature of archives as venues for knowledge production but also to think about our own, and others, engagement with them as researchers attempting to recreate new knowledges from these remnants of past lives and places. Considering our own archival practices and the ways we work, and would like others to work, with our past materials helps us to be more critically reflective about the range of questions and considerations required in the different stages of archival work.

EXPANDING THE ARCHIVE

Whilst the archive holds great weight and attraction for the majority of historical geographers, the expansion of interest in tracing the gaps and silences and further terrains of emotive experience, has led to an extension of archival research into people, places and environments that sit beyond traditional ideas of the archive. Lorimer (2009) notes that 'the spatialities and styles of archival research are still shifting' and many historical geographers are continuing to question their use of the archive and to develop new methods of practicing their archival work. The expansion of the archive comes in many forms including their geographies as digital archives turn our own living spaces into archival domains, changing the nature of our work with them and altering the stories written about our practice.

The expansion also considers different ways of acknowledging and developing historical geographical work. Sarah Mills (2013), for example, in her considerations of the fragments, objects and ghosts of the archive signals to the challenges of animating the archive and highlights the varied practices that are being utilised for engaging with archives (and the past). This notion of animating connects to wider calls for enlivening the archive through historical-cultural geographies, stressing the importance of expanding our understanding of what an archive can be and how we can work with it and its materials. The material and materiality become key components of thinking about such work connecting to wider calls across the discipline of human geography for accounting for the co-presence and physicality of the 'non-human' (or 'more-than-human'). Labelled the 'rematerialisation' of human geography, this shift has led to a number of new ways in which geographers, including historical geographers, have innovatively investigated the ways that social worlds and materials intertwine.

This can be powerfully seen in the seminal work of Caitlin DeSilvey (2007) where she tracks the entanglement of cultural and natural histories through the residual material culture of a derelict homestead in Montana. This work showcases how the notion of the archive can transcend human-made physical spaces and instead be considered as a place compiled with more-than-human matter. In this work DeSilvey is concerned with exploring issues of order and reordering, as discussed above, to ask important questions about our valuing of historical sources of knowledge. In doing so DeSilvey (2007, pp. 319–320) encounters a range of different matter:

> As I worked in the homestead's derelict structures, I often came upon deposits of ambiguous matter – aptly described by Georges Bataille as the 'unstable, fetid and lukewarm substances where life ferments ignobly' (1993: 81). Maggots seethed in tin washtubs full of papery cornhusks. Nests of bald baby mice writhed in bushel baskets. Technicolor moulds consumed magazines and documents. Repulsive odours escaped from the broken lids of ancient preserve jars. Rodents, moulds, insects and other organisms, long accustomed to being left alone, had colonized the excess matter. … I am not particularly squeamish, and I did poke, but the edge of revulsion was never far away. I worked close against the margin where the 'procreative power of decay' sparks simultaneous – and contradictory – sensations of repugnance and attraction (Bataille, 1993). In my early excavations, the degraded material presented a problem that I could barely articulate, let alone resolve.

Questions arise for DeSilvey around acts of recovery and decay in relation to these materials. Should she consider these junk or treasure? Should she seek to salvage these pieces of the past or allow them to degrade? This is a ground-breaking piece of work that seeks to present new orthodoxies for thinking about historic sites as it presents the idea of working with the decaying matter in its own form rather than attempting to salvage it. Through her research DeSilvey non-human matter as historical source, and the derelict landscape as her archive. She notes that she was able to read the messages on a wall of tattered newspaper scattered with box-elder seed, and to include rodents, insects and mould as part of her archival research. DeSilvey's work highlights the 'rediscovery of the material' in historical geography that has led to a rethinking of archival practice and a wider inclusion of what constitutes an archive in historical geographical research. We might similarly use these methods in other sites, such as the post-industrial ruin or an abandoned institutional space. The turn to the non-human might extend our historical geography reach to engage with places and landscapes beyond the archive.

This enlivened approach has led to a number of historical geographers to explore storying archival experience, in connection with Steedman's approach discussed above, to open up and examine different ways of considering the archive as a place of encounter. Merle Patchett (2019) recounts powerfully an embodied encounter between her students and a box from the archive marked 'FEATHERS.' She describes how the box of fashioned creatures, dead birds that would have once adorned hats, gave students the opportunity to reflect on the immediacy and materiality in front of them, placing them at the heart of archival practice. Describing the outcome of the workshop she notes:

> We arrived at this sense of care and custodianship in the workshop not simply through the intellectual exercise of relinquishing human exceptionalism but also by recognising our shared vulnerabilities as animals: the wearing of gloves being essential to protect not just the botched-bird bodies from further damage but to also protect our own bodies from traces of arsenic. ... For it was only through the botched-birds' mutual inclusion at not just at an intellectual level but also at a visceral and affective

level in the workshop that we simultaneously came to feel and care for the ways in which our histories – past, present, and yet-to-be – *coincide* with avian ones.

(Patchett, 2019, p. 653)

This collision between past, present and future histories in the storying of archival experience is a common returning theme across historical geography, illuminating the possibilities of what can emerge when we view and write our archival experiences as an embodied encounter. Uma Kothari (2021) explores the affective qualities of archives through her work with the Mission to Seafarers in Melbourne, Australia. She describes her work as unfolding as she searches through the discovered archives of the Mission in situ to uncover the changing relationships between ships and the sea, the city and seafarers. The documents, photographs and objects she was working with produced vivid and emotional histories, however, Kothari notes that there was something particular and important about working with the archive in the Mission itself. During her research she recounts how the rhythms and atmospheres of the Mission itself played an important part of her work, including the people who worked and passed through there who shared their enthusiasm and insight in the archive, thereby shaping the histories that were told. These affectual interactions are often missing in the recounting of archival work however as Ashmore, Craggs and Neate (2012) convey working-with archives in this way actively (re)shapes and (re)makes archival materials and the stories that emerge from them making them important and fascinating insights for our own research.

Through paying attention to the creative, enlivened and imaginative geographies of the archive there is rich potential for exploring new voices, places and experiences of the past that remain difficult to uncover. New ways of uncovering historical relations are brought to life through considering different materialities, such as more-than-human matter and auditory worlds (della Dora, 2021). Indeed, for those histories within living memory we might also be able to utilise oral history methods whereby we use interviewing methods to ask people about their pasts and memories. This entails its own challenges and similar questions regarding absences and presences emerge, but the push towards more creative and engaged methods, with a wider range of objects, places and voices, remains. We will return to exploring these aspects further in Chapter 5 where we will think in more depth about the ways in which researchers are working with their sources and the ethical implications for expanding and enlivening approaches.

BOX 3.3 Exercise – Enlivening the archive

In her work exploring the patient experience at Gartnavel Mental Hospital, Glasgow, in the 1920s, Hazel Morrison (2014) explored the dynamic approach to mental health care. As part of her research she worked with patient case notes from the hospital to explore patient-psychiatrist relationships.

Key to Morrison's approach was to understand the hidden patient experience and to try to uncover this from the archive. She used archival records of a hospital consultation recorded verbatim by a stenographer to think carefully about the experiential nature of the practice and the lived experience of the encounter.

Firstly, read (aloud) this extract from the case notes used in Morrison's work. Think about the ways in which you could work with these materials to research the patient voice.

Extract from Gartnavel Case Conference

(Q refers to the psychiatrist, M.O. the patient, and A another physician)

Simple Commands. (vocal)

Q. Put out your hand (A) Said "[indecipherable]", looked uncomprehendingly at M.O., did nothing.

Q Put out your hand.

(A) [Indignantly] "Where is the hound": Relapsed into murmurings.

Q. Put out your hand? (A) Nothing done.

Q. Rgt; 4 times (A) Looked at M.O., did nothing but continued looking for a moment.

Q. Put out your tongue (A) [pause] "Its out".

Q. Put out your tongue; Rpt 2ce (A) Oh for k- a little before I'll come

[indecipherable]

Q. Shut your eyes. (A) And what's that for.

Q. Rpt (A) And miss you walkin' ...

Simple Commands (vocal: reinforced.)

Q Put out your hand [M.O. hand held out]

M.O. had held patient by wrist, and she said "I must get some for my hands": after he said "Put out your hand" patient said with some affect "my hand's held out"

...

Q "Shake hands?" ...

A "Already (surprised) – is that the way you do?" Patient put hand out gradually against M.O.s held hand, but did not attempt to grip it...

Q Pause for suitable moment, then "Put out your tongue", M.O. put out his

A "Oh, no, - we all do that".

Q. Proceeded as before. "Put out your tongue".

A. ... "I don't think he'll put out his" _ stopped, seemingly on formation of word "tongue".

Q. As before "Put out your tongue".

A No response, patient looked away.

[An excited patient started shouting outside the door and then at the window – patient took almost no notice] ... repetition of question seemed to have little definite influence on the response. Source Reference: (1 Case no 468 GB812 HB13/5/185/3 NHSGGCA.)

Firstly, consider:

1. What does this extract tell you about the patient experience?
2. What are the gaps and silences that you can identify?
3. What challenges can you identify working with these materials?

Alongside using the written sources as evidence for her discussions of patient voice in Gartnavel hospital, Morrison also developed this work into a dramatised performance where actors voiced the 'script' of the meeting and explored the dynamics of the psychiatric encounter. This is another demonstration of the ways in which historical geographers are attempting to animate the archive.

How could you imagine working with this material in an enlivened way?

SUGGESTED READING

As identified in this chapter there are a number of directions you could take your reading on archives, depending on your interests and direction of research. We would encourage you to engage widely with these debates to help you to situate your thinking and expand your practice.

Hodder, J., and Beckingham, D. (2022). 'Digital archives and recombinant historical geographies', *Progress in Human Geography*, *46*(6), 1298–1310.

Kothari, U. (2021) 'Seafarers, the mission and the archive: affective, embodied and sensory traces of sea-mobilities in Melbourne, Australia', *Journal of Historical Geography*, 72, pp. 73–84.

Ogborn, M. (2011) 'Archive', in Agnew, J. and Livingstone, D.N. (eds.) *The Sage handbook of geographical knowledge*. Sage: London, pp. 88–98.

CONCLUSIONS AND THE IMPORTANCE OF CONSIDERING PRACTICE

This chapter has showcased a variety of ways in which historical geographers have considered the archive and archival practices. It has offered insights into the ways in which historical geographers have considered the archive and its role in structuring and shaping our research. Considering archives as different kinds of places has illuminated the complex power relations that are embedded within, and percolate through, our use of archives infiltrating our research in multiple ways. Furthermore, this chapter has introduced some of the sources used in historical geography research and highlighted the different ways in which their usage influence the narratives of research produced, even when widely on the same topic.

A key aspect of considering the place and role of the archive is to carefully consider our relationship to it. This chapter has illuminated our place in research and how our embodied selves are crucial components of archival work. Thinking about *practice* leads us to consider archive worlds where relationships between people, material and place are intertwined and continually shaping each other. Considering our emotional responses to our archive work, and to our encounters with the archive, is fundamental and raises a number of personal and ethical issues that we will discuss in Chapter 5. Highlighting the importance of incorporating issues of encounter into historical geography research this chapter has discussed the shifting nature of the

BOX 3.4 Hints and tips for working in the Archive

Visiting the archive for the first time can be slightly daunting and feel potentially overwhelming. This is not always the case, and many archives strive to make the archives as accessible as possible. Archivists themselves can be incredibly helpful and knowledgeable so do ask questions before (via email for example) and during your visit. Before concluding this chapter, we wanted to offer a few hints and tips from our own practice when visiting archives:

- Plan your visit. As noted earlier in the chapter it is really important that you contact the archive before your visit and book the materials you wish to look at. However, it is equally important to plan the logistics of your visit, for example noting what time the archives are open and closing, what documentation you need to access the reading rooms, and how will you get there are all important aspects of preparing for your research.
- Have an archival notebook (paper or virtual). Whilst perhaps obvious, having a set of notes that are exclusive to your archive visits can be extremely useful when returning to your archival work and thinking about writing.
- In this notebook you should look to record key findings, archival evidence (e.g. quotes) but also your own perceptions and ideas (these are often the beginnings of your analytical approach), In our experience, if these ideas are not written down then there is a risk they may be forgotten!
- With the permission of the archive, take photographs. This can be incredibly useful, particularly if you are time limited in your archival visit. That said, do not use photographs as a substitute for reading the archive. Thousands of photos are not particularly helpful unless you understand their relevance and how you might use them in the future.
- Where possible, talk to the archivist. They know the archive better than anyone and might be able to point you in the direction of other resources and materials. Sometimes catalogues and file request systems can be difficult to understand. Archivists can be incredibly helpful in familiarising yourself with their archives.
- Keep in contact. Always thank the archivist for their time and share with them the outcome of your research. For example, did you find out some key results from the archive and has the material inspired you to understand things in new ways. Sharing this with the archive helps others to learn from your work in the future.

archive to more enlivening terrains which we discuss further in Chapters 5 and 6 where we discuss issues of using source materials and writing historical geography.

What begins to emerge in our discussion is how the archive is a complex site shaped and reshaped by several actors (e.g. institutions, archivists, individual donors). As such, how we write about the past must recognise how the past remains in the present, and this generally requires engagement with the archive (which as we have seen can take many forms). Rather than positioning the archive as a site simply of historical truth, or neutrality, we have looked to consider the archive as a site of complex power relations and embodied encounters which shape how we revisit the past. Acknowledging how the past is constructed in your own context is important – are you grappling with the absences of your interest or instead working through an abundance of material? The examples provided begin to reveal several strategies for doing so, including triangulating your sources, recognising and working with the absences within your collections, and considering how your archive came to be. These are factors that you might wish to reflect upon in discussing your methodology (more on this in Chapter 5). The chapter has also revealed the influential role of theory in shaping our approach to the archive and we now turn more directly to the relationship between historical geography and theoretical approaches in Chapter 4.

REFERENCES

Ashmore, P.I., Craggs, R. and Neate, H. (2012) 'Working-with: Talking and sorting in personal archives', *Journal of Historical Geography*, 38, pp. 81–89.

Awcock, H. (2021) 'Stickin' it to the man: The geographies of protest stickers', *Geography Compass*, 53(3), pp. 522–530.

Baker, A.R.H. (1997) '"The dead don't answer questionnaires": Researching and writing historical geography', *Journal of Geography in Higher Education*, 21(2), pp. 231–243.

Baker, A.R.H. and Billinge, M. (eds.) (1982) *Period and place: Research methods in historical geography*. Cambridge: Cambridge University Press.

Bressey, C. (2002) 'Forgotten histories: Three stories of black girls from Barnardo's Victorian archive', *Women's History Review*, 11, pp. 351–374.

Bruinsma, M. (2021) 'The geographers in the cupboard: Narrating the history of Geography using undergraduate dissertations', *Area*, 53(1), pp. 67–75.

Clayton, D. (2021) ' Historical geography I: Doom, danger, disregard–towards political historical geographies', *Progress in Human Geography*, 45(6), pp. 1692–1708.

Cole, E. (2016) 'Blown out: The science and enthusiasm of egg collecting in the *Oologists' Record*, 1921–1969', *Journal of Historical Geography*, 51, pp. 18–28.

Craggs, R. (2008) 'Situating the imperial archive: The Royal Empire Society Library, 1868-1945', *Journal of Historical Geography*, 34, pp. 48–67.

de Leeuw, S. (2012) 'Alice through the looking glass: Emotion, personal connection, and reading colonial archives along the grain', *Journal of Historical Geography*, 38(3), pp. 273–281.

della Dora, V. (2021) 'Listening to the archive: Historical geographies of sound', *Geography Compass*, 15.

Derrida, J. (1996) *Archive fever: A Freudian impression.* Translated by E. Prenowitz. Chicago: University of Chicago Press.

Derrida, J. and Prenowitz, E. (1995) 'Archive fever: A Freudian impression', *Diacritics*, 25(2), pp. 9–63.

DeSilvey, C. (2007) 'Salvage memory: Constellating material histories on a hard-scrabble homestead', *Cultural Geographies*, 14, pp. 401–424.

Duncan, J. (1999) 'Complicity and resistance in the colonial archive: Some issues of method and theory in historical geography', *Historical Geography*, 27, pp. 119–128.

Ferriday, L. (2023) '"An indispensable aid": Urban mobility, networks and the guidebook in Bristol, 1900–1930', *Journal of Historical Geography*, 79, pp. 99–110.

Foucault, M. (2001) *The order of things: An archaeology of the human sciences.* London: Routledge.

Gibson, C. and Warren, A. (2023) 'Animating historical resource geographies: Encountering the guitar's North American material traces', *Journal of Historical Geography*, 81, pp. 110–122.

Gough, M. (2023) 'Representing Freetown: Photographs, maps and postcards in the urban cartography of colonial Sierra Leone', *Journal of Historical Geography*, 81, pp. 3–15.

Hartman, S. (2008) 'Venus in Two Acts', *Small Axe*, 12(2), pp. 1–14.

Heffernan, M. and Thorpe, B.J. (2018) '"The map that would save Europe": Clive Morrison-Bell, the Tariff Walls Map, and the politics of cartographic display', *Journal of Historical Geography*, 60, pp. 24–50.

Hodder, J. and Beckingham, D. (2022) 'Digital archives and recombinant historical geographies', *Progress in Human Geography*, 46(6), pp. 1298–1310.

Keighren, I. (2007) 'Breakfasting with William Morris Davis: everyday episodes in the history of geography', in Gagen, L., Lorimer, H. and Vasudevan, A. (eds.) *Practising the archive: Reflections on method and practice in historical geography.* Volume 40. Historical Geography Research Series: London..

Kothari, U. (2021) 'Seafarers, the mission and the archive: Affective, embodied and sensory traces of sea-mobilities in Melbourne, Australia', *Journal of Historical Geography*, 72, pp. 73–84.

Legg, S. (2025) 'Contesting monuments: heritage and historical geographies of inequality, an introduction', *Journal of Historical Geography*, 87, pp. 1–12.

Lorimer, H. (2009) 'Caught in the nick of time: archives and fieldwork', in DeLyser, D., Aitken, S, Crang, M. A., Herbert, S., and McDowell, L. (eds.), *The SAGE handbook of qualitative research in human geography* (pp. 248–273). London: SAGE Publications.

Maddrell, A. (2009) *Complex locations: women's geographical work in the UK 1850–1970.* RGS-IBG Book Series. Chichester: Wiley-Blackwell.

Mayhew, R. (2007) 'Denaturalising print, historicising text: Historical geography and the history of the book', in Gagen, L., Lorimer, H. and Vasudevan, A. (eds.) *Practising the archive: Reflections on method and practice in historical geography.* Volume 40. Historical Geography Research Series: London.

McGeachan, C. (2016) 'Historical geography II: Traces remain', *Progress in Human Geography*, 42(1), pp. 134–147.

Mills, S. (2013) 'Cultural–historical geographies of the archive: Fragments, objects and ghosts', *Geography Compass*, 7(10), pp. 701–713.

Morrison, H. (2014) *Unearthing the 'clinical encounter': Gartnavel Mental Hospital, 1921–1932. Exploring the intersection of scientific and social discourses which negotiated the boundaries of psychiatric diagnoses.* PhD thesis, University of Glasgow.

Naylor, S., Macdonald, N., Bowen, J.P. and Endfield, G. (2022) 'Extreme weather, school logbooks and social vulnerability: The Outer Hebrides, Scotland, in the late nineteenth and early twentieth centuries', *Journal of Historical Geography*, 78, pp. 84–94.

Norcup, J. (2015) 'Geography education, grey literature and the geographical canon', *Journal of Historical Geography*, 49, pp. 61–74.

Ogborn, M. (2011) 'Archive', in Agnew, J. and Livingstone, D.N. (eds.) *The Sage handbook of geographical knowledge.* London: Sage, pp. 88–98.

Patchett, M. (2017) 'Taxidermy workshops: differently figuring the working of bodies and bodies at work in the past', *Transactions of the Institute of British Geographers*, 42(3), pp. 390–404.

Patchett, M. (2019) 'Archiving', *Transactions of the Institute of British Geographers*, 44(4), pp. 650–653.

Philo, C. (1992) 'Foucault's geography', *Environment and Planning D: Society and Space*, 10(2), pp. 137–161.

Steedman, C. (2001) *Dust.* Manchester: Manchester University Press.

Stoler, A. (2009) *Along the archival grain: Epistemic anxieties and colonial common sense.* Princeton, NJ:, Princeton University Press.

Wideman, T. (2023) 'Archives and care: Caring archival research practices in geography', *Canadian Geographies*, 67(3), pp. 394–406.

Withers, C. (2002) 'Constructing 'the geographical archive', *Area*, 34(3), pp. 303–311.

HISTORICAL GEOGRAPHY AND THE VIBRANCY OF THEORY

INTRODUCTION

Historical geography is motivated by a commitment to uncovering the past, and attempting to tell stories with these pasts, illuminating hidden histories and uncovering previously silenced narratives. The stories uncovered however are not stumbled across by accident. This chapter reflects upon what drives our research and subsequent story-telling. It considers the role of theory in shaping our research commitments, questions and modes of analysis. Our central claim here, as demonstrated throughout the book, is that this is a distinguishing feature of historical geography, particularly in comparison to history. Historical geographers are noteworthy for their willingness to engage with theoretical approaches, something which we will unpack throughout this chapter. Much of this theory is connected to wider conceptual thinking within human geography around space, place and scale, whilst also drawing upon more structural and post-structural traditions and ideas. This connection between the empirics of the past and the wider, more translatable sense of theory, is what can make historical geography particularly fulfilling.

For historical geography then, theoretical approaches have become increasingly visible within scholarship whereby authors acknowledge how their use of historical materials is informed by concepts and ideas, whilst also using their material to shape new theoretical understandings. With this in mind, the chapter highlights the role of theory within historical geography. Indeed, it argues that this is a distinctive contribution of the sub-field. Rather than unpacking every theoretical approach in detail (each approach would merit

DOI: 10.4324/9781003483588-4

a *Basics* entry in their own right!), the chapter demonstrates how historical geographers have utilised theoretical tools to illustrate the diversity and vibrancy of theory within the discipline. To assist with this, the chapter starts with a story of a life from the archive, to reveal how theory might shape our research and the stories we tell about the past.

But before doing so, you might ask what is a theoretical approach? Put simply, theory can be considered as a series of more abstract ideas, distinct (yet deeply connected) from the empirical world of reality, that can be used to explain and understand the world. How you understand a place, event or life will be shaped by your wider approach to understanding the world around you. We might also consider it as a way of seeing through a particular lens. When thinking theoretically, these ideas tend to have some form of transferability, a sense that they are more systematic and translatable, rather than narrowly empirical, or contrastingly more speculative or random. Theory can allow for the identification of patterns and trends, providing explanations for shared experiences in different places and times. When revisiting the past, for example, you might well propose the relative significance of a particular factor in shaping an event or lean towards a particular story or life within your exploration of an archive. We provided some sense of this in the openings of Chapter 2, for example, where the increasing influence of feminist historical geographies and decolonising the past was briefly introduced. Both of these ideas are not specific to a time or place but instead are indicative of how theoretical principles might mould our research interests and shape the discipline more widely.

We constantly make small decisions in how we (re-)tell history and recognising the importance of theory leads us to question how we do so and how we might learn from other approaches. Thereby we theorise the past; applying an idea, concept or approach to history. Indeed, even our choice of subject, archive or participant is rarely a random one. Instead, our approach to history is driven by a commitment beyond the empirical. It might be a motivation to (re-)tell the lives of women, or an interest in the histories of race and racism, or perhaps an exploration of past movements driven by social justice. The telling of each of these will likely appear quite differently depending on how they are conceptualised and understood. In this regard, it is generally useful to distinguish conceptualisation from operationalisation. The two are deeply connected, but if operationalisation reflects the doing of research (see Chapters 3 and 5), then conceptualisation reflects the theoretical underpinnings of how we understand that research. It is the latter that this chapter turns to.

This may seem a daunting prospect. Some readers might prefer the tangibility of a case study. The ability to piece together what happened, where it happened and how it might be understood. Yet for others, and ourselves are included here, we share this interest in the detail of the past with an interest for wider, more transferable understandings of societal relations. How might one event or process be linked? Is there something translatable from one place or time to another? Theory offers some tools to make connections. But where do we start, are we to aimlessly scour the world of theory until we find our answers? Fortunately not, as rather than always being fuelled by a need to constantly create new theory (although this remains a possibility), human geography has a range of schools and traditions that might prove useful for revisiting the past. This chapter looks to introduce some of these, whilst also indicating the importance of this for shaping our engagements with the past.

As already noted in Chapters 1 and 2, historical geography has many distinctive features and has changed considerably over time in how it revisits the past. This chapter looks to focus in on the use of

---

BOX 4.1 Exercise – Selecting histories and considering theoretical influences

Take a moment to consider your historical interests so far. Perhaps you have a well-defined research archive ready to be explored, or maybe you've a more general idea of the past you wish to find. Either way, it is likely that your decision was likely informed by a more abstract commitment to a particular approach or way of thinking.

Task – Consider the following

1. What drew you to your historical geography interest?
2. How does that interest link with wider geographical ideas?
3. Are there any theoretical tools that you think might be useful for thinking about your topic? [don't worry too much if you're not sure on this final question, the chapter will explore this]

theory, highlighting how theoretical tools might assist in the study of the past. It argues that theoretical approaches shape and mould both our research interests and how we analyse and commentate on the past. Indeed, we must also recognise the wider range of ideas and schools of thought that might shape our approaches, including those beyond the anglophone influences that are dominant in our own account in this book. Ferretti, for example, has signalled the importance of what he describes as 'other geographical traditions' and here we acknowledge the work of Ferretti and the likes of Archie Davies (2018) who has strived to translate works (such as those from Brazilian geographers) into English to extend theoretical conversations within geography. Similarly, recent calls within the *Journal of Historical Geography* have called for further work into translation so to extend the exchange of ideas in a more international and multilingual manner (see Legg et al., 2025). These conversations are timely, and are very much ongoing, but we wanted to acknowledge these here so as to highlight the limits of our own reading of historical geography (as discussed in Chapter 1) and to encourage a widening of the lens through which you might approach theory within historical geography. Such conversations are central to wider conceptual debate within human geography, whereby questions are being asked about the history of the discipline as well as its future directions (see Cresswell, 2024).

Some examples are provided, and prominent theoretical schools noted, but you should not feel restricted by the theories identified here. Instead, look to reflect upon how you select and analyse your materials. As different theoretical traditions are unpacked below, we ask that you note their principles, nuances and distinctions. Each approach or concept might illuminate particular elements of the past but might also produce omissions and absences in doing so. Acknowledging this is important, whilst also identifying how empirical materials might make us rethink our theoretical approach. To help with this, our entry point for theory is through an individual life, and some exploration of the ways in which differing theoretical positions might foreground particular elements of that life. Following this, the chapter spends more time noting some influential and emerging theories from historical geography, to begin to show the influence of theory and the importance of it in shaping our analytical approach. This leads the chapter towards some conclusions around shaping research questions.

A WEST AFRICAN STUDENT IN A BRITISH UNIVERSITY – ROBERT WELLESLEY COLE

Robert Wellesley Cole was born on 1st March 1907, in Freetown, Sierra Leone. He was extremely well educated, first studying at Fourah Bay College before moving to the United Kingdom to study medicine at Newcastle University in 1928 (Figure 4.1). Arriving on to campus, he was 21 years old and would have been part of a small group of West African students studying in Britain, and likely an even smaller group studying in the North East region of England. International students are now a major part of university campuses in contemporary society and their lives are geographically pertinent in many ways. Geographers have reflected on student identities through studies of their experiences of mobility, engagements with cultural societies and processes of inclusion and exclusion within everyday life on our campuses. We can show similar historical geography interest in Cole as a mobile life, a young West African in North East

Figure 4.1 Newcastle University Campus.
Source: Shutterstock: Rachael Pinto.

England, and as a student of medicine who would go on to become a doctor within the British healthcare system. He would establish his own medical practice in Newcastle in 1934 and become the first West African to be a member the Royal College of Surgeons of England. His life is an important one for recognising the presence of West Africans, and people of colour more broadly, within early twentieth century North East England and might be part of a wider decolonising history project within cities like Newcastle.

Cole could also be described as an activist, retaining a strong link to Sierra Leone and African societal issues. He would work alongside other West African people in Britain to retain connections with the continent of his birth. His archives, held at the School of Oriental and African Studies, reflect these connections through his correspondence, memberships of societies (e.g. the West African Students' Union) and his involvement with transatlantic publications (e.g. as editor of *Africana* from his Newcastle home). His life, then, is of academic and public historical relevance, and is documented in two autobiographies – *Kossoh Town Boy* (1960) and *An Innocent in Britain* (1988). Here, we foreground his life as an important historical geography in its own right, but also as one that connects with several different historical geography theoretical positions. *An Innocent in Britain* is primarily used here as a source of wide-ranging relevance for historical geography study but also as a means to show the relevance of theory for approaching the past.

How we revisit his life, and his biographical story, can be shaped by the theoretical position we may choose to work from. Whilst the framing below might appear quite crude in places, and we are keen to emphasise the potential for utilising intersecting and multiple concepts and approaches, it helps indicate how theory shapes our research questions and our analytical approach. Four theoretical lenses are offered, namely reflections on postmodernism and understanding mobility, secondly an introduction to theory as associated with postcolonialism, thirdly a more specific introduction of solidarity and resistance as two more precise concepts and finally a reflection on institutional geographies. These are entry points, offered as a steer for how theory might be used to shape our research, and are certainly not introduced as an exhaustive account of possible approaches. There is much more beyond this, and you should read more widely to shape your own theoretical approach – consider for example how your other modules, wider reading or research interests might be considered through the past. Following this, the chapter considers some other theoretical developments within historical geography in recent times, before concluding with some more general reflections on the use of theory within historical geography and some guidance around the crafting of research questions.

POSTMODERNISM – GLOBAL LIVES AND NON-LINEAR BIOGRAPHY

Our starting point asks questions regarding how to write about a life and in doing so where we might start with Cole. Traditional biographical studies might emphasise a linear, chronological understanding. Person X was born, and they lived through a series of events and experiences before their life came to an end. The temptation therefore is to revisit these in chronological order on a fact-finding mission, piecing together a life in a linear manner. There is merit to this approach, and for many autobiographies (self-authored) and biographies (authored about someone else) are popular forms of reading and writing. Yet, this approach might not be the only way we think about an individual life. Historical geographers have increasingly viewed the individual through a variety of theoretical approaches, focusing in on a spatial approach to biography (see Chapter 6). This might stress the spaces and places of a life, it may also indicate a more relational understanding of time and space, zooming in and out, jumping backwards and leaping forwards, on moments and time periods. This troubling of space and time begins to lean towards a theoretical approach that can be broadly grouped together under approaches associated with postmodern theory, challenging assumptions and pointing to new directions. For Cole, this might lead us to encounter particular elements of his life.

In *Geographic Thought: A Critical Introduction*, Tim Cresswell (2024) gives time and attention to trends and shifts in geographical thought, noting in particular the evolution of approaches within human geography. One of the most notable, yet trickiest to define, is that of postmodernism. Perhaps confusingly, it is easier to start with what postmodernism is not before attempting to unpack what it might be. Cresswell notes how postmodernism is not necessarily a unified body of theory, indeed part of its associated principles are that there is no singular truth and that categories and approaches should be challenged. Notably, many of the authors that might be associated with postmodernism are unlikely to label themselves postmodernist. This immediately makes such a tradition difficult to define.

Yet the emergence of postmodernist thought is attributed to a particular moment in time and associated with a group of authors who have encouraged more relational, less rigid, conceptual thinking. It has also had significant influence on the discipline of human geography. Creswell notes, for example how postmodern thought, recognising in particular the influence of Edward Soja, pushed geography to more critical approaches towards a 'new geographies of difference', and as a discipline became increasingly influenced by the French philosophy of Michel Foucault and Jacques Derrida. This posed challenges to established approaches and questioned some of the categories, social distinctions and understandings of power that were established within the discipline.

This shift became increasingly influential in the 1980s and 1990s with a growing emphasis upon more relational thinking and the assertation that there are no fixed truths. This challenged previous approaches which set out to prove or disprove a theory or hypothesis. Returning to our interest in Cole and biography, it can be considered anti-essentialist and indeed useful for thinking about biography in a non-traditional manner as noted above. This suggests a move towards a more particularist approach in the study of experiences and relations, challenging orthodoxies. So, for Cole, we might consider his life as both *connected* through travel and friendships and *disconnected* through distance and exclusionary forces (particularly racism), as a West African student in Britain.

Cole's archives reflect his connections to an African diaspora, revealing how he became part of student societies and initiating new initiatives, yet equally they expose how his life was impacted by many processes of racialised exclusion in early twentieth century Britain. These dynamics were experienced across space and time but also intensely felt in moments where the layering of social difference fostered specific experiences. As such, we might view his life through the intersectional identities of race, class and gender, and likely beyond these social characteristics too. Through a postmodern lens we begin to view his life through a complex layering of social relations (which in themselves remain difficult to define) and a series of events and moments which might bear significance for his social experience. Crucially, the approach offered here allows for greater nuance in how these relations might be attended to and might trouble a simple, sequential ordering.

For biography, then, this poses a question for how we (re-)visit the individual life – not necessarily as a linear series of events and experiences, but as more of a relational account across space and time, through rhythms, connections and disconnections. For example, we may foreground how moments within a life might be intensely felt, as potentially connected to other moments, or how spatial elements might be analysed in greater detail, without relying on a simplistic linear framing of time. We could also think about biography as more performative, and as a research methodology experienced relationally by the researcher and the research subject. We become increasingly connected to the person we research as we strive to understand their life, yet at the same time we are always aware of the limits of our reach. As such, we can reflect upon how we go about this exercise and consider how we might look towards a more relational, spatial understanding of a life (McGeachan, Forsyth and Hasty, 2012).

Of more particular relevance here, is the more relational, pluralistic and experiential sense of mobility uncovered by geographers and other social scientists. Rather than viewing travel as mobility, framed simply as the travel from A to B, scholars have instead begun to interrogate the multitude of experiences associated with travelling as process. For example, Kim Peters (2015, p. 265) has stressed the potential for turning to maritime worlds to explore the spaces and experiences of the ocean, contesting some of the landed assumptions of geography:

> In other words, people aren't just mobile – they are mobile through particular typologies of motion – running, jogging, skipping, sliding, bumping. Each of these are experientially different. There is a need, therefore, to unpack the specificity of particular ways or methods of being mobile as each of these has its own cultural connotations, affective registers and political purposes. Mobility then, is not just about moving in a simplistic, one-dimensional fashion.

Her stress upon the experience of travel as focussing in on different versions of mobility is a helpful one. This leads us to our first entry point into Cole's life. We find Cole reflecting on the process of travel, particularly his time on board the ship which first brought him to Britain in September 1928. Rather than noting his place of destination (Freetown, Sierra Leone), or his place of arrival (first London and then Newcastle), we find him reflecting on the world of the ship, as a site where social difference was encountered and felt:

> Meanwhile we enjoyed the life on board. It was a reversal of the life on land which we had left behind. On land the Whites were few in and about the streets, and the whole scenery was Black faces. Here on board, the Black faces were our three, plus a handful of similar passengers from Ghana and Nigeria. The ship belonged to the Whites of England. Even the stewards and stewardesses were White. The Black non-passengers were down out of sight, in the engine room as firemen shovelling in the coal and mopping up the much. Otherwise they duty in the holds.
>
> The few Blacks sat at tables separate from the Whites. But of course there was no segregation, no apartheid. The Whites were armed with the frozen stare of a race who believed they were superior. But they did not look into our faces, and we did not look into theirs.
>
> [...]
>
> And, to confirm this, little things happened that made us real-ise that the iron platform we were floating on in our voyage to Blighty belonged to them.
>
> (Cole, 1988, p. 51)

As encouraged by mobility scholars and theorists interested in travel-ling as experiential (rather than instrumentally considering travel through departure and arrival), we find Cole reflecting on his experi-ence of mobility, a moment where he left Sierra Leone enroute for England. He spent two weeks onboard and we can only speculate the emotions of leaving home and the excitement and trepidation of approaching somewhere new. Not just anywhere new but a site deeply connected to home through colonialism (see Postocolonialism – representations of social difference). His reflections reveal much about the varied mobility experiences found on board the ship, not-ing how it was a 'reversal of life on land.' It is this moment of reali-sation that is found through the experience of travel.

We do not have space to fully unpack these reflections here but the approach shapes how we understand the life, and how we might situate a life within the worlds they inhabit. Here, Cole hints at several dynamics of the times. He identifies the power relations of the ship and the dynamics of race and racism, with the ship that 'belonged to the Whites of England.' He briefly recognises the black workers below deck, hinting at the hard labour and racialised exclusions faced by Black and Asian seafarers during these times (see Griffin, 2015; Griffin and Martin, 2021). These hierarchical relations were clear in the structures of the ship but they are also evident through smaller encounters and interactions, such as certain looks and gestures which indicated racialised difference. This produced an atmosphere which might be difficult to fully describe but his reference to 'little things that happened' will resonate with many in understanding the social relations found aboard the ship. This speaks to a politics of colonialism, race and racism that is found within the realm of the everyday, as well as within the more spectacular moments of racialised violence. There is much more to be said about these aspects of violence, and the themes are considered further below (Figure 4.2).

Figure 4.2 Seafarers and maritime space.

Source: Shutterstock: noraismail.

But for now, our starting point has introduced and questioned how we think about biography. Introducing postmodernism is no easy task and we recognise how this is a particularly complicated entry point. It is primarily introduced, though, to raise questions regarding how you are conducting research. How are you deciding what to include and exclude? How are you writing about social difference in your research, and the many layers of social relations that inform our study of events? This approach encourages the zooming in and out, the relational mode of geographical thought and how this then leads into some of the other interests too. Fundamentally, postmodernism is a broad approach, asking us to always challenge our assumptions and to consider alternative interpretations. This holds much in common (but also important differences and occasional disagreements!) with some of the other approaches and concepts introduced below, starting first with postcolonialism.

POSTCOLONIALISM – REPRESENTATIONS OF SOCIAL DIFFERENCE

During Cole's second year in Newcastle, the city hosted a large exhibition aimed towards revitalising industrial interests in inter-war Britain and specifically the North East region, which relied strongly on heavy engineering during these times. The North East Coast Exhibition ran from May to October 1929, and involved significant construction and landscaping of parts of the Town Moor (a large green space within the city). The event drew millions of visitors and was a large attraction within the region. Many of the buildings and features were only temporary constructions but the exhibition looked to showcase industrial innovations, sporting activities, arts and culture, whilst also illustrating Britain's international influence through the British Empire. The international links of events like this were reflected in many ways, and at other similar exhibitions (often named 'Empire Exhibitions') in the late nineteenth and early twentieth centuries in cities like London and Glasgow. The event took place during Cole's time in the city:

> That summer an international North East Coast Exhibition was held at the vast Newcastle Town moor. It was well supported by the business community of the North east. Among the side

attractions proposed and advertised in the months in advance was an 'African Village'. I was shocked at the idea. Doherty, Koi, and I wrote vainly to the local papers against the idea. The thought of displaying these people in a zoological side show in this strange cold country, to be an object of ridicule and entertainment, was objectionable.

(Cole, 1988, p. 81)

Cole and his fellow students were appalled by what they discovered. The African Village had become an integral part of Exhibitions during these times and often included the deeply troubling spectacle of human exhibits, claiming to represent African society and allowing audiences to watch for their entertainment. The previously dubious sense of such exhibits as holding educational, anthropological value had long been discredited from the late nineteenth century. The extract above is troubling in many ways and highlights a little known history of colonial relations as found within Britain, as opposed to those found within colonial territories. It raises several questions regarding how we might write related histories and how best to revisit such moments. The chapter now turns to an introduction to postcolonial theory to move forward this mode of inquiry.

Postcolonial theory has become increasingly influential within human geography, recognising the continuing influence of colonialism within and beyond previously colonised nations, as well as continued forms of colonialism within contemporary society and forms of neocolonialism and imperialism. Put simply, post-colonialism (note here with a hyphen) might refer to those times after colonial rule but as should become clear postcolonial theory (note here without a hyphen) has a much deeper and sophisticated interest in the pasts, presents and futures of colonial influence. Much of this theoretical work has pushed historical geography to revisit past lives, events and processes through a postcolonial lens. There is a need to reflect on the power relations of the past which made colonial violence possible, whilst also reflecting on the postcolonial worlds which shaped lives within and beyond the metropole. Such thinking pushes us towards a more critical analysis of the power relations which shaped colonial domination and subaltern resistance, alongside that which might be found in-between. Tariq Jazeel (2019, p. 19) provides some useful introductory reflections for those looking to conduct such work:

> It has been about a dialectics of learning from the marginal and marginalized. It has involved working against blithe generalizations, and it has sought ways of situating difference in its own geographical and historical problem spaces. Another way of putting this is that postcolonialism is incessantly preoccupied with context; a word (con-text) whose etymology implies the weaving together of texts, of textiles in fact, precisely in order to fabricate. In this sense, it is worth reiterating postcolonialism's close relationship with post-structuralism and its insistence on transcending faith in the existence of rigid, bounded structures, such that we might instead glimpse the ways that what appear to us as structures are always, in fact, in the process of being (re)made, dynamically, textually.

Jazeel notes many points of interest here, which might also be applied to the experiences of Cole above. He points to the 'marginal and marginalized' as important for geographical study as well as stressing how postcolonial scholars might consider the dynamics of colonial contexts, crucially framing the structural relations as dynamic, contested and multiple. This is important for troubling simplistic assumptions and instead considers the layering of colonial relations across society, through texts, representations and daily interactions. In short, postcolonial scholars are concerned with hybridity as opposed to singular interpretations. In doing so, scholars like Jazeel draw attention to key postcolonial theorists such as Edward Said and Gayatri Chakravorty Spivak and showcase how their work has continually engaged critically with the politics of representation (particularly through text and image) which reinforced the power dynamics of colonialism, and how such constructions sat alongside the violences and direct domination of colonial rule. These representations continue to hold influence and reoccur in contemporary forms of media and culture (Figure 4.3).

It is with these threads in mind that we might revisit Cole and his fellow students' life experiences. After less than a year in Britain, Cole is confronted with the prospect of an African Village, supposedly displaying what newspapers described as one of the most well

Figure 4.3 Exhibition Park Newcastle – building remaining from the 1929 Exhibition.

Source: Shutterstock: Hazel Plater.

attended amusements and by the end of the exhibition over half a million people had paid to see North African natives go about their 'daily life':

> [The] 'African Village' was engaged with by schools across the region and it was reported that over the course of the exhibition some 150,000 schoolchildren had visited in organised parties.
>
> (*Hartlepool Northern Daily Mail*, 26 October 1929)

In his autobiography, Cole describes his shock and objection at the 'zoological' representation of Africa. His response is important in several ways. He draws attention to a part of the exhibition that might otherwise be missed in accounts of visitor numbers, positive accounts of the spectacle and visitor testimony. He also indicates the ways he attempted to voice his concerns (more on this below), and how local newspapers refused to publish these. With these threads in mind, we can begin to reflect upon how colonialism and race was represented in Britain, and notably here in North East England. This is important for troubling false assumptions around cities like Newcastle for holding a less cosmopolitan history than other British cities (such as London and Liverpool).

In short, Cole's account draws attention to a little-known history (specifically the African Village) and highlights a much wider post-colonial history, not confined to Sierra Leone (the place where he was born) but through a far more relational sense of place within and beyond Newcastle. When viewed through a postcolonial lens, we might situate the African Village within a wider set of relations in the North East region at this time. Cole would likely be aware of many of these dynamics as he began to explore the university, city and wider region. Hannah Martin's (2021) PhD thesis highlights many of these dynamics, noting, for example, 'race riots' in South Shields in 1919 and 1930 between white sailors and sailors from Yemen. She also identifies the presence of problematic representations of Empire as found within everyday life in North East England, such as through media, marketing and advertising.

In attending to multiplicity, as encouraged by postcolonial theory, we might also suggest that there are other, more hopeful, stories to tell. Cole was exposed to processes of 'othering' and discrimination (as noted elsewhere in his biography and see below for reference to his time working within the National Healthcare System), yet his life and archives are also evidence of a multicultural experience that was more inclusive and international. His archives reflect a series of collective endeavours to bring communities together, including his involvement with student societies and international groups. These engagements were sustained beyond his studies and present throughout his life. He would write and edit publications, attend meetings, travel with groups across Africa and participate in events such as those hosted by the West African Students' Union (WASU). Jazeel (2019, pp. 4–5) describes postcolonialism as more of a methodology than a theory in that it is attentive to the spatial-temporal dynamics of colonial relations. This includes researching times and events after colonialism (with hyphen), the legacies and continued influence of colonialism (without a hyphen), but also postcolonialism as a move towards imaginaries and world making beyond the limits of colonial thought. Doing so is to highlight a plurality of experiences, illuminating the abuses of African villages and misrepresentations of Africa, but also reflecting an alternative vision and representation of African society through Cole's own participation in groups and societies.

RESISTANCE, SOCIAL JUSTICE AND ACTIVISMS

Postcolonial theory, then, pushes us to think of "missing" others, alternative perspectives and the politics of representation. It asks questions regarding the influence of colonialism, how it was felt historically and how it persists in the present. It is undoubtedly helpful for further justifying the revisiting of Cole's life and highlights how we might reflect and unpack it in the 1920s and 1930s. In this next section, we pick up a particular thread of Cole's life to narrow our focus further. As hinted at above, these representations and troubling forms of racism and 'human zoos' were contested. Cole and his peers wrote in vain to their local newspapers to protest the event. This is indicative of the potential for resistance and links with a long running interest for human geography scholars. Whilst Cole's letters were never to appear in the local press, he was aware of a more established organisation that was able to contest the African Village:

> Fortunately there was in existence a Union of West African Students of Great Britain and Ireland, which had been formed a few years earlier, and was under the active management of Mr Ladipo Solanke, Nigerian barrister, ex-Fourah Bay student. He had remained in England, where in London he carried on his work and interests on behalf of Africa. He took up the matter urgently, and the idea of getting such people from British Africa was scrapped, thanks to help from sympathetic members of Parliament.
>
> (Cole, 1988, p. 85)

This little-known story is important for how we understand events. There might be a tendency to assume the African Village occurred with little opposition or concern. However, Cole notes several perspectives that disagreed with the Village and actively contested it in the weeks and months prior to the Exhibition. As such, including the alternative voices and practices of resistance remain important for retelling this historical event from 1929. In order to better understand such efforts we might turn to human geography's interest in social justice movements and conceptual understandings of resistance and solidarity. These works have shown how power relations, including those of colonialism and capitalism, have been resisted in diverse way.

Paul Routledge (1997, p. 69), for example, has consistently offered an emergent understanding of resistance, framing it 'to refer to any action, imbued with intent, that attempts to challenge, change, or retain particular circumstances relating to societal relations, processes, and/or institutions.' This definition is helpful as it opens up how we might understand oppositional acts, introducing ideas around intentionality and how resistance might generate other alternative practices. As Hughes (2020) has identified, resistance intentions might not necessarily reflect the longer trajectories or neatly map onto the outcomes of resistance. A more flexible definition of resistance is again helpful here and acknowledges how domination and resistance might not always be easily distinguished as binary categories. Similarly, David Featherstone (2012, p. 5) defines solidarity 'as a relation forged through political struggle which seeks to challenge forms of oppression.' He helpfully unpacks solidarity in three distinctive ways, firstly as 'transformative relation,' secondly, as a 'practice that can be forged 'from below,'', and thirdly, as indicative of the 'refusal of political activity to stay neatly contained within the nation-state.' Such introductory definitions are indicative of a more relational approach to social justice, and also a much wider field of study, which within historical geography has looked to explore oppositional politics, campaigns against injustice and the fostering of solidarity. Crucially, for thinking about the role of the approach these works have explicitly stressed a geographical understanding of these movements and activisms.

Taking these pointers as conceptual guides, we can begin to analyse the efforts of Cole, and the West African community more generally, in contesting dominant societal processes. The 1929 Exhibition was a large-scale event that had significant investment and support from local and national government. It was confronted by resistance to the plans to host an African Village, though, and WASU campaigned against its presence. The student union of West African students would go on to protest the conditions of workers during the 1938 London Exhibition. In 1929, their campaign would lead to the issue being discussed in Parliament, with Member of Parliament (MP) Shapurji Saklatvala raising the issue:

> though it may not be repugnant to the exhibition authorities here, or to the British visitors, it is very repugnant to the educated section of Africans, and does he not further realise that we are only making an exhibition of the wretched way in which citizens are reared up and kept in the British Empire?[1]

The campaigning efforts of the student society were given leverage through a Communist Party MP who took their cause for political debate. The shared frustration towards this deeply racialised form of human abuse had effects, although not to the extent that they wished, leading to The British Government intervening and preventing the use of human exhibits from the British Empire. Yet, the event's organisers were able to bypass any restrictions placed upon them by utilising their own global connections to exhibit Senegalese people (at the time a French Colony) as part of their 'African Village.'

The village remains deeply troubling and reflects attitudes amongst festival organisers and attendees at the time. Yet, the presence of an alternative voice of resistance, as drawing attention to the case of social justice, remains significant. It indicates that there were alternative views and collectives that actively opposed such representations. This requires remembering. Geographers have continually stressed the importance of attending to social justice campaigns and the power dynamics of social, political and economic processes. Here, their words and conceptual tools might again be useful. The efforts of students to oppose the African Village should not be dismissed despite the eventual continuation of the event. Their oppositional voices and actions reflect a dynamic of anti-racism that has a much longer history within Britain. Recognising their activities then allows us to attend to the spatial politics of their resistance that connect with a longer temporality of related struggles. Hughes (2020) points to this by highlighting how 'there is value in keeping the future open' and attending to the many possibilities shaped through acting in resistance. It might be that such framings become relevant for your own study, whereby you can utilise the works of human geography to revisit past organising efforts, campaigns and demonstrations. Next, we turn to a theoretical approach to understanding institutions as linked to the earlier discussion of carceral space mentioned earlier in Chapter 2.

INSTITUTIONAL HISTORICAL GEOGRAPHIES

As Philo and Parr (2000) note, geographers have become increasingly interested in the institutional. In Chapter 2, we introduced prison spaces as sites where institutional dynamics of care and control are found. Prisons are responsible for the enclosure of space for the imprisoned, as a direct and indirect form of control, but are also generally responsible for some level of rehabilitation, which might be thought as care. These dynamics have long fascinated geographers but as carceral geographers have been keen to stress (Moran, 2015), these dynamics are not limited to prisons. Surveillance, monitoring, and conditioning are found within many different environments and particularly institutions such as schools and hospitals. Historical geographers then, have been increasingly interested in such spaces and aim to consider the experiences of being in and associated with such spaces. Philo and Parr (2000, p. 518) point to how human geographers (and historical geographers) might engage with institutions, recognising how:

> attention does indeed get directed to the existence, composition and possible mutation of the institutions themselves, to their internal timings and spacings, as much as to any external effects that they might have in other spheres of the human world (even if any hard distinction between the inside and the outside of an institution becomes rather scrambled in the process).

These relations within and beyond the institution are indicative of a relevance not only to the prison as mentioned in Chapter 2 but several other settings. They might also be found in education and healthcare where the dynamics of care and control are also prominent. These are institutions which are designed to create the conditions through which it could be possible to 'improve human minds and bodies' (Philo and Parr, 2000, p. 513). How these spaces are studied is generally informed by an understanding of power and space, reflecting on what Foucault describes as a method which challenges assumptions and pushes us towards a questioning of the making of norms and institutional roles. He calls on scholars:

> To show that things "weren't as necessary as all that"; it wasn't as a matter of course that mad people came to be regarded as mentally ill; it wasn't self-evident that the only thing to be done with a criminal was to lock him up.
>
> (Foucault, 2020, p. 226)

This historical questioning of institutional (and other) makings of power relations is crucial for how we might revisit the past lives of institutions. Foucault's emphasis upon power relations, as a more complex entanglement of processes and practices, begins to reveal the makings of institutions such as hospitals, schools and prisons. It also questions their supposedly objective and scientific nature or to assume progressive intentions. Instead, he offers a more nuanced analysis of how power operates in these spaces and questions assumptions about them. As noted in Chapter 2, his thinking might encourage, for example, a critical exploration of the dynamics of care and control within these spaces, and trouble the more simple framing of these dynamics.

This troubling of the role of institutions is important and introduces a more critical lens for our understandings of institutional spaces. It might allow us to attend to the relationships between staff and subject, between those inside and outside, and also to understand the role of the state in shaping institutions. As noted in Chapter 2, attending to the micro here might reveal something about the macro. This was again true in the life of Cole following his graduation as Doctor and subsequent experiences of looking for work. What he encountered was a healthcare system that held institutionally racialised attitudes and approaches. In a letter to the then Secretary of State for Health, Nye Bevan, he documented his struggles in searching for work in North East England:

Letter dated – 12th April. 1948.

After a student career which ended with my heading the list of Finalists, and a postgraduate period of specialised training which lasted ten years, I not only hold all the recognised surgical qualifications, namely the Mastership of Surgery (Durham) and the Fellowship of both the Royal Colleges of England and Edinburgh, but I have now been put on the Consultants Rolls of the British Medical Association. Only one thing I have never been able to achieve, namely a Hospital Appointment, so necessary for the proper practice of my speciality.

(Cole, 1988, pp. 273–274)

The letter began by documenting his difficulties in finding employment within healthcare settings and continued by describing how following an agreement to conduct surgery at a Newcastle practice, he received a letter shortly after that withdrew the opportunity:

Two mornings later, however I received this letter:

Dear Sir, with reference to our telephone conversation of yesterday. I find we are so busy we cannot undertake work for any more surgeons. Thanking you, S. Mahane, (Matron).

[…]

I pointed out that I was a bona fide Consultant (that is one practising solely as such), that I was on the Consultants Roll, that in the absence of any previous intimation or any written evidence her ruling had the appearance of an 'ad hoc' decision, and that in point of fact I was probably the only Consultant surgeon in Newcastle who would suffer under the terms of the ban.

[…]

I need only add that I am a West African, was born at Freetown, Sierra Leone, and that my family have been British for over a hundred years.

(Cole, 1988, pp. 273–274)

Cole's letter is revealing in many ways. The timing of which is also important. The National Health Service was established in July 1948 and UK healthcare became centrally organised through National Government. At the same time doctors such as Cole were unable to find work due to the decisions of matrons, as administrators, at particular hospitals and nursing homes. Cole is keen to point out in his letter that this reflects a longer pattern of behaviour in his search for employment and desire to progress his career. His experience begins to foreground the social and spatial dynamics of institutions that stretch beyond the walls of the places themselves and have profound impacts on the experiences therein. Indeed, Cole's experience would more than likely be considered an example of institutional racism in contemporary times. As such, thinking through the dynamics of institutions remains highly relevant for our pasts, presents and futures. Historical geography has been particularly attentive to the spatial dynamics within these institutions, the relations of care and control which might be found within them, and the connections with wider societal forces (such as race and racism) which shape people's experiences within them (whether as staff, service user or visitor).

BOX 4.2 Exercise – Robert Wellesley Cole – Feminist historical geographies?

The approaches offered so far have centred Cole through his experiences, words, worlds, and life stories. Some theoretical possibilities for doing so have been introduced. Yet, it is also worth noting that Cole's sister would become a doctor too. Seemingly, though, there are less materials relating to her life. Cole himself acknowledges Dr Irene Ighodaro in his autobiography. He notes how she did particularly well at Annie Walsh Memorial Girl's School and that he helped her in accessing the opportunity to learn in England. Rather than pursue a career in education, as had been assumed by many, Irene asks to attend medical school. She was successful:

> She fulfilled the matriculation requirements and entered the Newcastle Medical School in October 1938, ten years after I had left home. She qualified in 1944, the year before the end of the war. She was the first Sierra Leone woman to qualify as a doctor, the second West African. A Nigerian lady had preceded her by a couple of years.
>
> (Cole, 1988, p. 159)

Whilst not limiting feminist historical geographies to the lives of women, and acknowledging gendered relations and their influence more broadly, there is something significant here to explore further (see McDonagh, 2018). Dr Irene Ighodaro would have experienced many of the same dynamics that her brother did but would have had different experiences too. She was born in Sierra Leone in 1916, registered as a doctor in 1944, and held her own medical practice. One might ask how her life can reveal something different to her brother. We might ask how a feminist geographer would look to uncover her biography, and understand her geography.

Your exercise here, is to consider your research questions if Irene was to become the focus of our research. A feminist historical geography might insist that we do so, as to avoid her life is to ignore a vital perspective on the times. There is more on research questions to come in this chapter, but for now consider what elements of her life you are interested in. This might connect with the perspectives offered on Robert as discussed above, but might also extend to new places and dynamics.

List up to three research ideas/questions relating to Irene and feminist geographies (other approaches might remain relevant here).

In concluding our discussion of Cole and theoretical entry points, we can begin to acknowledge the possibilities for theory to reveal how there are many stories to tell of an individual life. Crucially, this is not distinctive to individuals or biographies, as the same could be said of an event or place-based history. How we choose to go about this is important and theory offers us tools to navigate the past. In continuing this chapter, we now look to draw out some wider theoretical traditions that have been particularly influential within historical geography. We pay attention to the diversity of theoretical influences within the sub-discipline. As ever, this list is not exhaustive but does begin to illustrate the diversity of theory within historical geography, as well as revealing the conversations which emerges when holding theory alongside evidence from the past.

HISTORICAL GEOGRAPHY AND THEORETICAL APPROACHES

How we revisit a life then, from a historical geography perspective, is shaped by how we theorise our research interests. Similarly, theory will shape how we research events and moments and what we choose to illuminate in our story telling. It also begins to offer some comparability of our findings, through the translatability of theory and the potential for comparison – whereby experiences from one place in the 1920s, might be connected to ideas emerging in the 1980s, because of how theory shapes our understanding and how we think about events and processes. So far, the chapter has looked to show the value of theory through an empirically informed manner. What follows next, is a summary of some emergent theoretical areas within historical geography. These are not exhaustive but are indicative of the continually evolving nature of the discipline and how we think and research the past. We start with some extended comments on historical geographies and the environment as an area of pressing research interest, before providing a series of shorter summaries of a wide range of other theoretical approaches that are increasingly influential.

ENVIRONMENTAL HISTORICAL GEOGRAPHY

Given the pressing nature of the climate crisis, and the unavoidable impacts of climate change globally, historical geographers have been challenged to consider their role in informing how we think about the environment. Historical geographers have much to offer in thinking about climate change, bringing methods to understand past climates as well as understanding the knowledges and cultures which shaped it. Increasingly then, historical geographers have worked in partnership with climate scientists, often found within the same departments, to consider how we might better understand past environments as a means to gain insight into the present and future forms of environmental change. How they do so is again theoretically informed and driven by contrasting approaches. Before surveying some other theoretical approaches, we thought it important here to acknowledge the growing importance of this body of work.

Matthew Hannaford (2025) notes historical geographies significance in his unpacking of environmental historical geography and describes three broad approaches that have been found in thinking through the geographies of environmental pasts. These include:

- Environmental reconstruction
- Environmental knowledges
- Environmental impacts

He notes how historical geographers have contributed to an understanding of environmental pasts by tracing environmental events and histories. This includes the study of weather events and changes in climate in places with the potential to model and understand longer histories of environmental change through both quantitative and qualitative historical sources. He also identifies historical geographers efforts to engage with different environmental perspectives, working with participants and archives to trace and illuminate the different understandings of the environment. This might trouble assumptions and approaches found in the Global North for example, and instead offer alternative insights into how the environment, and associated processes, are understood. For example, Aporta and MacDonald (2011) describe the process of gathering Inuit knowledges in Canada through the Iglooik Oral History Project, which looks to centre a stronger social and cultural understanding of the meaning of climate change. Finally, Hannaford (2025) identifies how historical geographers have attended to the impacts of environmental change and how a longer temporality of tracing these changes can be important. As an example of this, we might recognise the histories of community adaptation in the face of changing environments, including natural disasters and the daily challenges of a changing climate (e.g. drought, agricultural challenges, flooding and displacement).

These approaches are empirically orientated, in their attentiveness to processes of environmental change, but are equally theoretically informed. The efforts to illuminate alternative perspectives (through oral histories for example), or to revisit particular moments of environmental impacts, might well be driven by some of the theoretical impulses as described above. One can imagine a project on historical environmental change being driven by postcolonial and decolonial theory for example, or another project an environmental hazard centring feminist perspectives. That said, more broadly environmental historical geography, as part of the history of science, has also shaped its own theoretical approach, as one that centres geography in understanding the emergence of scientific practices. Here, we pay brief attention to this body of work as a means to further encourage engagement.

David Livingstone (2003, p. 1) has been particularly keen to stress the relationship between the spatial and the construction of scientific knowledge. Put simply, he argues for a renewed recognition of the interactions between place and science. Challenging the notion of an objective, placeless laboratory, he proposes that place is central to scientific practice:

> Scientific knowledge is made in a lot of different places. Does it matter where? Can the location of scientific endeavour make any difference to the conduct of science? And even more important, can it affect the content of science? In my view the answer to these questions is yes.

In doing so, he has formed a foundational part of a shift within historical geography towards a critical questioning of the production of knowledge, particularly that knowledge which presents itself as scientific. In this regard, there might be crossovers with some of the approaches mentioned above. There are immediate crossovers with postmodernism's questioning of truths, and postcolonialism's questioning of power relations in the production of colonialism (much of which was expressed as intellectually driven and territorial expansionist, though 'scientific' means). This questioning of the production of science then becomes significant for how we might reflect on historical geography possibilities. There is now a growing body of work that takes such questions seriously, with Simon Naylor (2005) helpfully surveying much of this scholarship. Naylor's (2024) own work has similarly considered the significance of place for understanding science, for example in his study of meteorological observatories in the nineteenth century, where observatories become experimental sites of science. Through engagements with archives and writings, he is able to explore the socio-cultural processes and geographies that have shaped scientific discourse.

Away from the historical geographies of science, more recent work has taken forward approaches towards understanding past environmental events. Academics in Hull, England, have looked to revisit flooding events through archival records, but have done so in a way that actively looks to engage with the present. McDonagh et al. (2023) have explored Hull's experience with the nearby River Hull and Humber Estuary to document nearly 500 years of living with water (1260–1700s). They use a variety of sources, such as

Figure 4.4 The Humber Estuary.

Source: Shutterstock: Neil Mitchell.

newspapers, Paten Rolls and reports from the Commission of Sewers. In doing so, they reveal a series of events (such as spring tidal floods) and decisions (such as Lord ordering the sluices to be broken to flood surrounding lands), which reflect centuries of town and environment interaction (Figure 4.4).

The academics involved with this work have not only produced deep historical readings of these events and forms of environmental planning. They have done so with a clear steer towards the present and an emphasis upon engaging contemporary audiences and connecting past and present interests, concerns and ambitions. Elsewhere, the project team have stressed the importance of this:

> Moreover, the potential of place-based, historically-informed approaches to drive action for climate empowerment has not as yet been adequately interrogated, and this despite the fact that city planners and global policy makers interested in nature-based and 'slow water' solutions are increasingly drawing on past water management practices as models for contemporary schemes. Crucially, none of these projects have made explicit use

of pre-twentieth century histories of living with water and flood in order to drive climate resilience actions today.

(McDonagh et al., 2023, p. 92)

In arguing this potential, the authors draw attention to their work through their use of public art projects, community engagement programmes and outreach alongside wider conferences and events (E.g. United Nations Climate Conference). Such an action orientated, public facing and participatory framing, looks to enliven the past through engagement with the present (see Chapter 3). This approach is in itself theoretically informed by a commitment to more actively position academic work in conversation with publics and draws upon a longer tradition of 'participatory' and 'public' geographical scholarship, including considerable debate about the challenges of doing so (see Fuller, 2008).

There is a long tradition of this sort of participatory work more generally and the salience for historical geography is hopefully quite clear. Earlier chapters have stressed the potential for the past to be considered 'usable' and this more participatory framing is where these principles are perhaps most apparent. Such projects reveal the potential for historical geographers to contribute towards contemporary debates, including climate thinking as noted above (see also Chapter 7). The past might reveal changes in community responses and uncover approaches to adapting within a changing climate, long before more recent debates. Such scholarship might be deemed even more significant in an era defined by climate crisis. Like before, though, this work is driven by theoretical underpinnings which utilise and explore the past with connections to wider geographical thought (for example how understand concepts such as risk, adaptation and resilience). In this regard, the approach to the past is transferable beyond the environmental applications as noted here.

THE VIBRANCY OF THEORY AND WIDER APPROACHES

This chapter has utilised the life of one person as a means to show the possibilities found within theory. The chapter has shown different entry points for understanding historical geographies. Hopefully, the notion that was initially introduced, of how the approach you choose to take will influence the stories you tell is beginning to become more apparent. The chapter also noted that it would be an impossible task to fully explore the theoretical breadth of historical geography and the disciplinary history of geographical thought more broadly. This will require some wider reading and critical thinking, and your topic might fit with the perspectives offered so far or further scoping of literature might still be required. To help with this, some wider schools of thought are briefly acknowledged here.

One area that has yet to be stressed is that of cultural geography. Cultural theory has had a profound impact on the social sciences and humanities more widely, and geography is no exception. The work of scholars such as Raymond Williams, Stuart Hall and Paul Gilroy have had significant influence. These scholars have shaped understandings of key terms that have become cornerstones of human geography and formed approaches towards cultural elements within life – including race and class, representation and media and politics and society. These works have stressed a more critical engagement with the power relations of representation, the conditions within which events occur and the multifaceted makings of social relations. For example, in relation to race and society, Stuart Hall has stressed the importance of the 'specific conditions' that makes racial characteristics 'socially pertinent' and 'historically active' (Hall, 1996, p. 52) in contrast to approaches that might simplify racism to singular, simpler economic reasoning.

Cultural geography has overlapped with historical geography in many ways, but arguably most notably through ideas of landscapes and this points us towards some wider theoretical schools that are worthy of some comment here. Landscape has been considered in multiple ways with the emphasis falling in contrasting directions (Wylie, 2007). Whilst there is scope to focus on the more-than-human within these landscapes, and many historical geographers have done so (Forsyth, 2013), here we briefly comment on the work of two approaches that have looked to reinsert the human within landscapes which can sometimes approached with omissions in their representations of nature.

Rural historical geographies provide a helpful starting point for thinking through landscapes. They are multifaceted and wide-ranging with entry points ranging from individual experiences of wandering and experiencing nature, to more critical approaches that include social difference and the political economy of landscapes. Rachel Hunt has stressed both dimensions, with her work on Bothies in rural Scotland, identifying a working-class experience within a space assumed to be the reserve of elites. She contrasts her approach to the rural with those singular, simplistic framings of the rural idyll:

> Work that charts the counter idyll and highlights its fractures upon social lines is perhaps more useful here in pushing rural geography forward. Halfacree (1993) was early to highlight that the rural idyll was the visioning of a hegemonic bourgeoisie and thus authors have since been at pains to emphasise the existence of 'other rurals' such as the Plotlanders of 1930s England. It is these 'neglected rural geograph*ies*' (Philo, 1997*emphasis added*) that I turn attention to, focusing on their ability to move us beyond the rural of 'Mr Averages'.
>
> (Hunt, 2019, p. 220)

Her work is important for challenging assumptions of rural space. She questions who informs our understanding of the rural for example, who has access to the rural and what experiences of the rural might look like. She utilises records from Bothy books and oral histories to compile an alternative historical perspective on the rural landscape. In doing, she uncovers a rural Scotland that is characterised by what she describes as a radical counter-rural presence, specifically through people's experiences that trouble the assumptions around these spaces, including a more diverse group of people walking, inhabiting and experiencing the rural. This approach is driven by a critical historical geography of the rural that uncovers other perspectives within the rural landscape (Figure 4.5).

Another challenge to our understanding of the landscape can be found through the work of a scholar such as Don Mitchell who explores rural landscapes with attention towards the political economy, specifically critiquing a particular form of cultural geography:

> More than from labor, much cultural geography is disconnecting itself from a concern with material spaces, sometimes arguing

Figure 4.5 Santa Ynez, California – a landscape which could be understood in many different ways.

Source: Shutterstock: Carolin Sunshine.

that since "brute reality" is unknowable, cultural geographers should concern themselves with how landscapes are only representations, only ideology. I think this is a misguided project.

(Mitchell, 1996, p. 4)

Here we begin to gain insight into the strength of debate found within human geography. A sense that one school of thought might steer the discipline in one direction at the arguable detriment of others. As already noted in Chapter 2, Mitchell specifically challenges a form of cultural geography that he suggests has moved away from questions of labour and inequality, and towards a less tangible, and perhaps more abstract questions of representation, experience and landscape aesthetics. In contrast, his own approach borrows from a school of Marxist geography, whereby questions of capital, labour and uneven power dynamics are centred through an approach characterised as historical materialism. This school of geographical thought has been particularly influential in shaping the discipline more widely (see Cresswell, 2024). In more empirical terms,

Mitchell's work has engaged closely with agricultural labour and the labour processes that built the rural landscape, specifically in California, highlighting for example the experiences of migrant labourers, the inequalities associated with their wage labour and the racism they encountered. Such an approach might hold wider relevance for the historical geographer in other contexts and could be linked to studies of working-class experience, control and resistance within workplaces, class conflict and the political economy of the histories of capitalism.

These approaches present contrasting interpretations of landscapes, with one centring cultural rural experiences and the other exploring broader dynamics of political economy. They both point towards different framings of power relations within experience of the past. In that regard, much of the theoretical discussion presented here asks us to question the power relations latent within the archives, and other pasts, we encounter. They are only acknowledged briefly here to illustrate wider theoretical interests as found within historical geography, and to further illustrate the plurality of potential approaches and how these might steer your story telling. Borrowing from some of the postcolonial influences previously mentioned, we might identify further historical geography scholarship that has taken these ideas away from British contexts and towards former colonial territories. Such theorisation has been at the centre of historical geography scholarship in revisiting colonial pasts.

Drawing on Michel Foucault and others, for example, Stephen Legg (2009) has explored the production of scale through his work with the archives of the League of Nations and the colonial Government of India, revealing specifically how dynamics of internationalism played out in relation to efforts to manage prostitution and trafficking in the early twentieth century. His work considers how these approaches were complex, territorial and imagined across different 'scalar apparatus'. Similarly, Sneha Krishnan (2023) has drawn upon feminist and postcolonial perspectives to explore the experiences of marginalised communities and populations, specifically young women and girls, within colonial contexts. Her work unpacks the contradictory dynamics of international connections and constraints on young girl's lives through development discourse in South Asia. More broadly, these works are acknowledged here as further perspectives which might be considered in your attempts to frame your own work. They are indicative of the constantly evolving nature of historical geography, pushing the sub-discipline towards different voices and new perspectives, and are suggestive of further theoretically informed directions that the historical geographer might take. If something noted here begins to resonate with your own ideas then consider finding the associated reading from the reference list or take a broad starting point with a wider theoretical take on human geography (see Cresswell, 2024).

A recognition of power and the archive have been touched upon previously (see Chapter 3), but what is clear from all the examples above (from understanding environments, to practicing science and understanding landscape) is that issues of power are central to much of historical geography thinking. This is also reflected across previous reference points in this chapter, which have foregrounded the power relations of colonial representations, the power dynamics of institutions and the power of resistance and social justice movements. Each of these centre upon the spatial dynamics of power in different ways. In this regard, historical geography has pushed us to think critically about power and its relational qualities in the histories we encounter. How we theorise these dynamics and the ways we revisit the past is a more complex process than what we might first assume, and some recognition of our approach is required in our writing (see Chapter 6).

THEORY, ARCHIVES AND RESEARCH QUESTIONS

Thus far, the chapter has introduced the role of theory for historical geography. Hopefully, it has shown the diversity and vibrancy of theory within the sub-discipline. Generally, your research projects will require a literature review which frames your study, both theoretically (with discussion as suggested above) and empirically (with some context for your study). We provide some further guidance on the writing of historical geography in a later chapter (see Chapter 6), but here our concluding point is to reflect on the shaping of your research questions. This is because of the close connection between theory and research approach. The opening examples introduced different elements of Robert Wellesley Cole's life and indicated how theory might illuminate particular elements of his life. At the same time, there was a suggestion that some elements might be stressed more than others. This recognition of the strengths and limitations of your approach is crucial for framing your research, indicating both what you are doing, but crucially placing limits on the scope of your study.

Writing research questions is difficult and may require considerable reading prior to fully narrowing your focus (for more on this see Peters, 2017). Theory is helpful for refining your approach. It points towards where your interests lie, how they connect to other work, and might place some interests beyond the scope of your project. In this regard, your research questions can be helpful for making your project manageable and feasible. In the case of Cole, it may allow you to focus on historical geographies and particular conceptual interests, rather than simply rewriting his entire biography. Generally, your study might have an overall aim and then a series of more specific research questions. In reference to the biographical example raised above, an overall aim might be:

> A historical geography study of an African Student on Tyneside: the life of Robert Wellesley Cole.

The aim is broad and gives a sense of direction. The example above identifies the sub-discipline of historical geography, an interest in an individual life, alongside the primary subject and place of study. This is a useful starting point as it identifies broad areas of interest. Yet, it doesn't really give a sense of specific interest or where the writing make take the reader. This makes the research questions important. Research questions follow from the overall aim and are designed to identify a more specific set of questions to be explored. Here, there is recognition that the overall aim is a broad one and that your study might not include every possibility which it hints at. Instead, your research questions might narrow your focus towards a particular angle of study. This is where the theory becomes increasingly influential in shaping your approach. For example, a project might be specifically interested in the dynamics of race and racism (perhaps shaped by postcolonial theory) in interwar Britain might ask the following:

- How was everyday racism experienced by a West African student in inter-war Britain?

- Where were the spaces and places within which racism was an active social force?
- How was race and migration represented in North East England during this period?

Whilst a study of the historical geographies of science, medicine and health institutions might ask:

- To what extent were migrant worker perspectives visible within the archives of the National Health Service?
- To what extent were medicalised spaces inclusive in relation to social differences?
- What strategies did people of colour develop in navigating their roles within the healthcare system?

And finally, a study of activisms and social movements (shaped by theoretical approaches to power and resistance) in the same period might consider:

- What strategies were used in efforts to oppose the 1929 African Village?
- What networks and solidarities were forged through this opposition?
- How was the opposition in 1929 connected to a longer trajectory of early twentieth century anti-racism in North East England?

Each set of research questions requires a different approach to the research. They emphasise certain elements as opposed to others and will narrow in on particular parts of Cole's biography and archive. The questions above emphasise some of the following principles for shaping your historical geography research practice which might be transferable to other studies and the writing of research questions.

Below we indicate some research question principles which might help you in shaping your own historical geography research questions:

- Be specific in what you wish to explore (identify the time period, subject(s) and location)

- Look to include geography (an interest in space, place, landscape and environment is important for the historical geographer)
- Indicate your specific interests (such as activities, attitudes, behaviours, etc.)
- Keep questions short and simple (they should be accessible and easily understood)
- Try to avoid double questions (add another question if required)
- Avoid closed questions which can be answered simply yes or no (e.g. questions beginning with 'do' and 'are')
- Avoid assumptions (e.g. 'how frustrated was Cole with the 1929 North East Exhibition?' – this assumes a response before even beginning your research)

Generally, researchers might identify an overall aim of their study and then sub-divide this aim into simpler research questions (generally 2 to 4 are recommended). Research questions can be theoretical, methodological or empirical. They might blend some of these elements together but should generally be more open and flexible in nature. You are also less likely to hypothesis test in your study. Instead, as a historical geographer, you are likely to focus on complexity and nuance. Some hints and tips towards doing this are provided below.

BOX 4.3 Exercise – Writing your research questions

Several of the exercises so far have asked you to establish your research interests. As you move forward with this, and perhaps once you've identified your sources (whether archives, oral history participants or other forms of access to the past), you should consider your research questions. These will frame what your project will operationalise, and crucially place limits on the scope of what you can achieve.

- Your task – write 3–4 research questions following the guidelines above. In doing so, consider how your theoretical approach shapes your research interests.
- Share these questions for feedback – with your peers, a supervisor or mentor.
- Rewrite, fine tune and edit the questions.

CONCLUSIONS

This chapter has covered a lot of ground. We have jumped from briefly introducing what is theory, to some theoretically informed dives into the life of Robert Wellesley Cole, before opening things out to reveal the vibrancy of geographical thought and some prompts for shaping research questions. In this regard, the chapter has the potential to be the most overwhelming of the book. This is not our intention and nor should the chapter be read in this way. Instead, our main motivation for writing this chapter in this way is to illustrate the possibilities offered by theory. These stretch beyond what is considered here and our examples, alongside the unpacking of ideas, are offered to encourage you to do the same. This will become increasingly clear in subsequent chapters, particularly around working with historical material and then writing with historical material.

In considering theory, several possibilities have been introduced, and these approaches hold rich potential for further exploration. The chapter started with an introduction to postmodernism and non-linear biography, before exploring some influences from postcolonialism and then narrowing to a more specific discussion of practices of social justice and solidarity, as well as institutional geographies. We then introduced environmental historical geographies before briefly surveying a range of schools and traditions. The chapter does not intend to be an exhaustive list, but perhaps you have been intrigued or inspired by a theory introduced here or alternatively you want to pursue gap or an oversight that has become apparent. Either way, theory should be present in your historical geography study. This may be lighter touch engagements across some related works or a deep exploration of a particular theorist or set of theories. You should always look to be attentive to how others have included theoretical reflections in their research. Most simply, you are likely to include a literature review in your essay, project or dissertation, and this might include some theory and context, but it might also emerge in your analysis and conclusion too (more on this to come!).

SUGGESTED READING

Depending upon your theoretical approach, you are likely to require a different set of readings. With this in mind, our two suggestions below are more general texts that introduce a variety of perspectives and approaches. These should lead you towards further prompts and ideas for shaping your theoretical approach:

Cresswell, T. (2024) *Geographic thought: A critical introduction*. Hoboken, NJ: Wiley Blackwell.
Peters, K. (2017) *Your human geography dissertation: Designing, doing, delivering*. Los Angeles: Sage.

NOTE

1   House of Commons Parliamentary Papers – HC Deb 08 May 1929 vol. 227 cc2185-6. Comment from Mr Shapurji Saklatvala.

REFERENCES

Aporta, C. and MacDonald, J. (2011) 'An elder on sea ice: An interview with Aipilik Inuksuk of Igloolik, Nunavut', *The Canadian Geographer/Le Géographe canadien*, 55, pp. 32–35.
Cole, R.W. (1960) *Kossoh Town Boy*. Cambridge: Cambridge University Press.
Cole, R.W. (1988) *An innocent in Britain*. London: Campbell Matthews.
Cresswell, T. (2024) *Geographic thought: A critical introduction*. Hoboken, NJ: Wiley Blackwell.
Davies, A. (2018) 'Milton Santos: The conceptual geographer and the philosophy of technics', *Progress in Human Geography*, 43(3), pp. 584–591.
Featherstone, D. (2012) *Solidarity: Hidden histories and geographies of internationalism*. London: Zed Books.
Forsyth, I. (2013) 'The more-than-human geographies of field science', *Geography Compass*, 7(13), pp. 527–539.
Foucault, M. (2020). *Power*. London: Penguin Books. [Online]. Available at: https://www.penguin.co.uk/books/23075/power-by-foucault-michel/9780241435083 [Accessed 9 August 2024].
Fuller, D. (2008) 'Public geographies: Taking stock', *Progress in Human Geography*, 32, pp. 834–844.
Griffin, P. (2015) 'Labour struggles and the formation of demands: The spatial politics of Red Clydeside', *Geoforum*, 62, 121–130.
Griffin, P. and Martin, H. (2021) 'The 1919 '"race riots"' – Within and beyond exceptional moments in South Shields and Glasgow', *Political Geography*, 88, Article 102408.
Hall, S. (1996) 'Race, articulation and societies structured in dominance', in Baker Jr, H., Diawara, M. and Lindeborg, R. (eds.) *Black British cultural studies: A reader*. London: University of Chicago Press, pp. 16–60.
Hannaford, M. (2025) 'Environmental historical geographies', *Geography Compass*, 18(12), e70013.

Hughes, S. (2020) 'On resistance in human geography', *Progress in Human Geography*, 44(6), pp. 1141–1160.

Hunt, R. (2019) 'Neglected rural geography: Exploring the quiet politics of "out-dwelling"', *Environment and Planning C: Politics and Space*, 37(2), pp. 219–236.

Jazeel, T. (2019) *Postcolonialism*. London: Routledge.

Krishnan, S. (2023) 'Ideal girls for Christian internationalism: The YWCA in early twentieth-century South Asia', *Social History*, 48(1), pp. 17–42.

Legg, S. (2009) 'Of scales, networks and assemblages: The League of Nations apparatus and the scalar sovereignty of the Government of India', *Transactions of the Institute of British Geographers*, 34(2), pp. 234–253.

Legg, S., Ding, Y., Ferretti, F., Morin, K. and Novaes, A.R. (2025) 'Historical geographies: Translating times and spaces', *Journal of Historical Geography*, 88, pp. 5–6.

Livingstone, D.N. (2003) *Putting science in its place: Geographies of scientific knowledge*. Chicago: University of Chicago Press.

Martin, H. (2021) The intersection of race, class and politics in the North East of England, 1919–1939. Doctoral thesis, Northumbria University.

McDonagh, B. (2018) 'Feminist historical geographies: Doing and being', *Gender, Place & Culture*, 25(11), pp. 1563–1578.

McDonagh, B., Brookes, E., Smith, K., Worthen, W., Coulthard, T.J., Hughes, G., Mottra, S., Skinner, A. and Chamberlain, J. (2023) 'Learning histories, participatory methods and creative engagement for climate resilience', *Journal of Historical Geography*, 82, pp. 91–97.

McGeachan, C., Forsyth, I. and Hasty, W. (2012) 'Certain subjects? Working with biography and life-writing in historical geography', *Historical Geography*, 40, pp. 169–185.

Mitchell, D. (1996) *The lie of the land: Migrant workers and the California landscape*. Minneapolis: University of Minnesota Press.

Moran, D. (2015) *Carceral geography: Spaces and practices of incarceration*. London: Routledge.

Naylor, S. (2005) 'Introduction: Historical geographies of science – Places, contexts, cartographies', *The British Journal for the History of Science*, 38(1), pp. 1–12.

Naylor, S. (2024) *The observatory experiment: Meteorology in Britain and its empire*. Cambridge: Cambridge University Press.

Peters, K. (2015) 'Drifting: Towards mobilities at sea', *Transactions of the Institute of British Geographers*, 40(2), pp. 262–272.

Peters, K. (2017) *Your human geography dissertation: Designing, doing, delivering*. Los Angeles: Sage.

Philo, C. and Parr, H. (2000) 'Institutional geographies: Introductory remarks', *Geoforum*, 31(4), pp. 513–521.

Routledge, P. (1997) 'A spatiality of resistances: Theory and practice in Nepal's revolution of 1990', in Pile, S. and Keith, M (eds.) *Geographies of resistance*. London: Routledge.

Wylie, J. (2007) *Landscape (key ideas in geography)*. London: Routledge.

5

WORKING WITH HISTORICAL MATERIALS

INTRODUCTION

Following on from previous discussions relating to the archive and practicing historical geography, this shorter chapter centres on exploring in more depth aspects of working with historical materials. Due to the practical nature of the content this chapter will draw less on other sources from the discipline and instead work with a key case study example relating to criminal-medical historical geographies to show different practices and tools in action. Following this, the chapter will also consider other ways of working in historical geographies by again drawing upon our own work to show how oral histories might similarly inform our research. Connections will be made back to Chapter 3 to highlight further the implications for a turn to considering 'doing' historical geography. Questions relating to what can be considered as historical sources will be introduced with reference made to the different ways of working that these generate and inspire. Finally, the chapter will reflect on issues of ethics and how fundamental these can be for our working with historical sources. Throughout the chapter you will be further introduced to the importance of critically reflecting on method and practice for shaping your research.

As previously shown, working with historical materials can be challenging with many historical geographers discussing the difficulties, uncertainties and unease over knowing how to work with the archival materials they are faced with. Similarly to other qualitative methods, such as interviewing and ethnography, there is no manual or one-size-fits all model for working with every source and this can

DOI: 10.4324/9781003483588-5

be a daunting moment for any researcher, particularly those starting out on their first historical project. As Chapter 3 highlighted there are a wide range of sources that can be drawn upon in historical work, ranging from texts to animals, objects to people and each will require a way of working that is nuanced and particular to the stories being written. This chapter aims to create a space for sharing reflections on working with historical sources, noting that there are multiple ways these could be diversified and/or challenged. An exciting aspect of working with historical sources is the multiplicity of interpretations and practices that can be tried out and utilised. There is no singular way of interpretating sources, just as there is no definitive version of the past that you are trying to tell. Whilst there are no set steps to follow for every project there are points of similarity across practice and the final part of the chapter aims to highlight these for your own further reflection.

ENCOUNTERING THE ARCHIVE

I (McGeachan) vividly remember the first time I caught sight of a particular historical source. I was attending an event at the University of Glasgow where a number of archival institutions from across the city had come together to showcase their collections. As I wandered curiously amongst the myriad of stalls, I glanced down at a table of old-looking notebooks, the squiggly handwriting catching my eye, and walked over to take a closer look. At the centre of the table, a large leatherbound notebook had been propped open and reading its opening line got me instantly hooked: 'At 5 A.M. on the 8th June I was asked to see a man "who was either dead or dying" as the messenger stated' (RCPSG 10/9/12). I later learned that this source belonged to Sir William Macewen, a prominent Scottish surgeon from the nineteenth century who amongst an almost unbelievable set of achievements was renowned for the first successful removal of a brain tumour. Yet, I had never heard of him. Whilst the source captivated my attention, my engagement with it was a multifaceted process, highlighting the range of, often unexpected, journeys our historical research can takes us (Figure 5.1).

After my initial chance encounter with the notebook, I wanted to know more about the context of the source and who it belonged to. I began by sharing my curiosity with the archivist on the stall, Ross

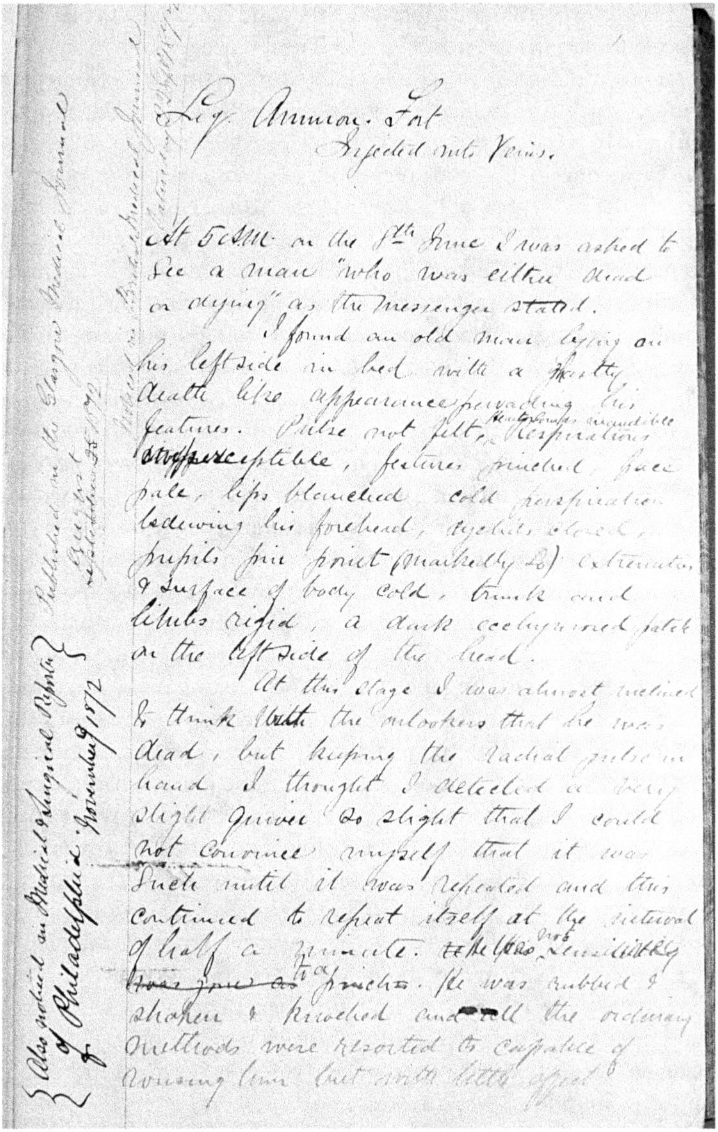
Lig. Ammon. Fort[illegible]
Injected into Veins.

At 5 A.M. on the 8th June I was asked to see a man "who was either dead or dying" as the messenger stated.

I found an old man lying on his left side in bed with a ghastly death like appearance pervading his features. Pulse not felt, heart sounds inaudible, Respirations imperceptible, features pinched, face pale, lips blanched, cold perspiration bedewing his forehead, eyelids closed, pupils pin point (markedly so) extremities & surface of body cold, trunk and limbs rigid, a dark ecchymosed patch on the left side of the head.

At this stage I was almost inclined to think with the onlookers that he was dead, but keeping the radial pulse in hand I thought I detected a very slight quiver so slight that I could not convince myself that it was such until it was repeated and this continued to repeat itself at the interval of half a minute. He was not sensible when pinched. He was rubbed & shaken & knocked and all the ordinary methods were resorted to capable of rousing him but with little effect.

Also noticed in Medical & Surgical Reporter of Philadelphia November 9 1872

Published in the Glasgow Medical Journal [illegible] 1872

[illegible] British Medical Journal [illegible] 1872

Figure 5.1 Private Journal of Surgical Cases, October 1873.

Source: RCPSG 10/9/12.

McGregor, who told me about Macewen and the range of collections relating to him that were held at the Royal College of Physicians and Surgeons of Glasgow (RCPSG). I asked more about the individual source, which was entitled Private Journal of Surgical Cases, and was intrigued to hear that the archivist had selected these works to bring to the event due to his own interest in the marginal nature of them. During the early years of his career in the 1870s, Macewen had been a police surgeon in Glasgow, and the notebook was his own personal account of his time working in this role. A police surgeon in the nineteenth century was a new and evolving position that fused together criminal investigation with medicine, becoming a precursor to the forensic officer we have today. Yet, little is known about the role and what it consisted of. The archivist had spotted this small array of sources in the larger archive and identified that nobody had used these in research before, highlighting a hidden aspect of Macewen's story.

This set of encounters demonstrates that from the outset my engagement with this source was a collaborative enterprise. Working with sources often means working with their owners and understanding and respecting these sets of knowledges and expertise is crucial. My follow-up engagement with the source took place in the reading room of the RCPSG. I had prepared for my visit two weeks beforehand by contacting the College and booking my space, noting what I wanted to look at and enquiring about any permissions that might be needed. With my pencil and notebook in hand I took my seat in the quiet reading room and stared at the journal that had been carefully laid out in front of me, propped up by a plump white cushion. Viewing the handwriting up close humanised Macewen as I instantly visualised a person writing his experiences of the world, a connective force between myself and the subject. Taking an exploratory approach, my first steps were to read the writing contained in the source to learn more about Macewen and his police surgeon experiences. As I began to read the document, I transcribed the piece in my own notebook, paying attention to deciphering words I struggled to read or make sense of, and carefully noting the reference and page numbers I was using:

> At 5 A.M. on the 8th June I was asked to see a man "who was either dead or dying" as the messenger stated.
>
> I found an old man lying on his left side in bed with a ghastly death like appearance pervading his features. Pulse not felt, heart

sounds inaudible, respirations imperceptible, features pinched, face pale, lips blanched, cold perspiration beading his forehead, eyelids closed, pupils pin prict (markedly so), extremities & surface of body cold, trunk and limbs rigid …

This stage I was almost inclined to think with the onlookers that he was dead, but keeping the radial pulse in hand I thought I detected a very slight quiver, so slight that I could not convince myself that it was such until it was repeated, and this continued to repeat itself at the interval of half a minute …

He was stated to have taken opium and when I entered the house a number of pill boxes presented themselves on the table near the bed, marked 'Opium pills'

(RCPSG 10/9/12 GB 250 10/9/12, Private Journal of Surgical Cases, 1872 – 1875, Sir William Macewen, (1848 1924), surgeon).

Slowly I began to piece together the story of what was emerging from the source. The case reports that Macewen had been called out to a person's home to deal with an emergency medical situation in June 1872. It reports upon a man's near-death condition due to opium poisoning and Macewen's administration of emergency medical treatment, a new (and clearly experimental) treatment of intravenous ammonia, which he had previously been testing on animals, to stimulate the vascular and nervous systems.

At the end of my first visit to the archive I had collected more questions about the source than answers, and I noted these in my fieldwork diary:

I found it interesting getting to know about Macewen as a police surgeon in Glasgow and performing experimental treatments. Why was he so experimental? What medical experiences had inspired him? What was it like for him going into people's homes and treating people in distress? I find myself drawn to thinking about the man that he treated, what is his story? What were the circumstances that led to his overdose? What happened to him afterwards?

(Visit to RCPSG, October 2017)

There are clearly two key aspects that stood out for me after my initial engagement with the source and the first one is geographical – what are the historical geographies of the police surgeon? As a historical geographer I am naturally curious about the geographical dimensions to sources and seek to make connections across different concepts and ideas within geography. I was struck by the mobile nature of Macewen's role, as from reading the journal it was clear that he was going out to different parts of the city to treat people in situ. This felt unusual to me, in relation to normal surgical practice, and made me reflect more deeply on the connections between the concept of mobility and the police surgeon. I wanted to know more about *where* Macewen went and what this could tell us about the geographies of crime and medicine in the period. The journal also led me to reflect more deeply on issues of place. Macewen describes the environment of the man's home that he visits when he arrives there, giving rare insight into the patient's intimate worlds which are often wholly absent from accounts of traditional practice. Macewen's description of the man's bedside cabinet and the atmosphere of his room draws attention to the importance of considering place in relation to understanding the complexities of the experience Macewen is writing about, taking into account the relationships between the place of encounter within the home and wider socio-economic forces.

The second aspect relates to my curiosities about the patient and his experience. As a researcher my philosophical foundations sit within humanistic traditions leading me to be drawn to phenomenological questions of lifeworlds and individual human experiences (Laing, 1965). Years of researching and trying out different kinds of philosophies and theories have led me to understand where I can position myself and my approach and whilst it can feel difficult and sometimes overwhelming to finding your philosophical bearings, they become an important compass for exploring historical sources. My interest in the individual patient stems from these foundations but also my theoretical positionings as a feminist historical geographer, an approach which values the stories of individuals and pays attention to marginal voices of experience.

All of these questions led me to the next stage of working with historical sources. Rarely do historical geographers work solely with one source and often it is within the triangulated use of multiple sources that we start to unravel the layered nature of the stories we are uncovering. Due to the uncatalogued nature of this part of Macewen's collection I was unable to look up any connections

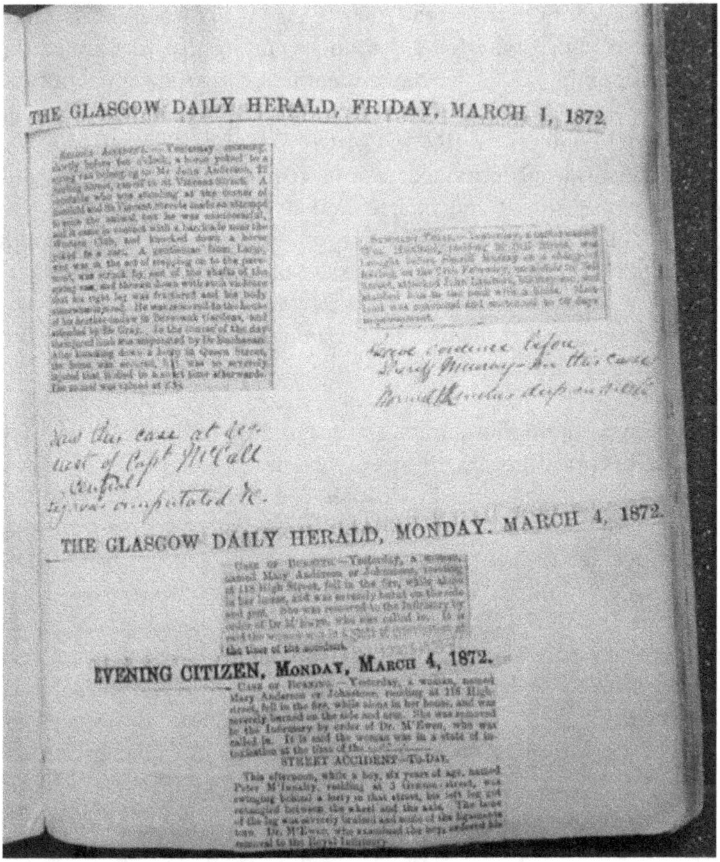

Figure 5.2 Macewen's Medical Scrapbook, 1872–1874.

Source: RCPSG 10/9/10A.

between sources online and again turned to the expertise of the archivist for advice on what other sources were available. The archivist noted that the collection also contained scrapbooks of newspaper articles that Macewen had collected and compiled during his time as a police surgeon (Figure 5.2).

These were delicate sources that required thoughtful handling and my approach to working with these became investigative as I was keen to dig deeper into the story from the journal and to try and find connections between the sources. As I read through the various snippets of glued-on articles, I found a cutting that mentioned the original opium case. The source identified certain details about the man mentioned, 'David Thomson, a warper, 69 years of age, residing at 203 High Street' (RCPSG 10/6/4/1-19 GB 250 10/9/10A). These small details provided an important window in the personhood of the patient and offered new avenues of exploration into David himself, including his place of residence and social worlds through his occupation. The article also provided details of the afterlife of Macewen's encounter with David and his medical interventions, as shortly after the treatment David regained consciousness but died after being admitted to hospital.

As previously noted in Chapter 4, theory shapes our encounters with the past providing important scaffolding to develop the shape of our historical geography research. Drawn to feminist historical geographies as described in Chapter 2, I was keen to develop this work in alignment with feminist theories that seek to challenge traditional (male-dominant) histories regarding crime and medicine, and to illuminate marginalised voices and experiences. I was very aware when engaging with these sources that they were written and produced by a white man of privilege and whilst I recognised and valued the significance of these histories my theoretical positionings moved me away from researching the stories of Macewen. Instead, I paid attention to those individuals whom he encountered, such as David, that are often lost to history. I began to go through each article individually in the scrapbook, taking careful notes of particular themes that connected with my key research interests, such as mobility, practice and marginal lives. As noted in Chapter 4, research questions and aims shape how we use our sources as we become attuned to different themes and ideas. I therefore took notice of certain places that Macewen visited, such as homes, city streets, shops, police cells and the work he undertook there such as examining bodies, assessing wounds or administering drugs. I also made notes on all the fragments of lives that appeared in the scrapbook, from people's names, their age, addresses, occupations, marital status and anything particular about their worlds that were mentioned in the pieces. This included aspects of their relationships, their socio-economic status, health conditions and past experiences with the law and medicine. My interest in

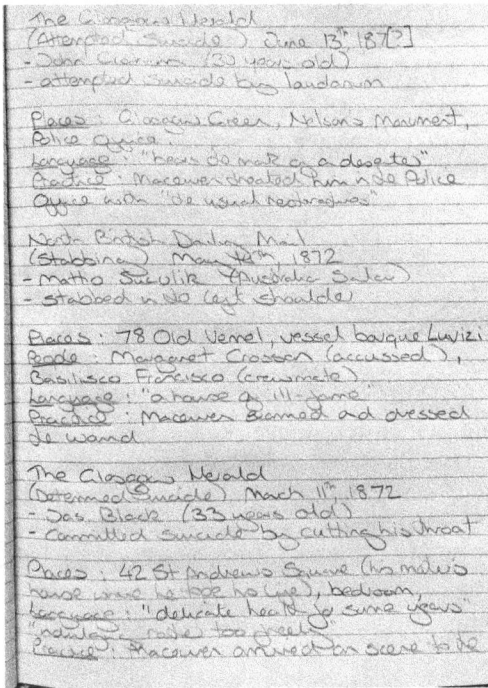

Figure 5.3 Notebook.

Source: author's own.

crime also led me to assess the sources for any information they could give me relating to criminal activity or the incident that was being reported leading me to compile a detailed list of violent activity (Figure 5.3).

This process of research led me to compile a body of data that spoke to my key themes, and I firstly sought to consider how I could use this data to generate a bigger picture of Macewen's mobility and practice. In conjunction with archivists and the digital heritage officer at the RCPSG, Kirsty Earley, we used the data compiled to create a map of all the cases that were mentioned and where Macewen encountered them in the city. In doing so we could show vividly the unusual practices of mobility that are present in the police surgeon's practice which had gone unnoticed in previous scholarship relating to the topic. Importantly for my historical geography research it brought to life a number of key geographies relating to Macewen's practice.

The research process also revealed a host of individuals who had been subjected to violence, sometimes physically by others or structurally by the state. I noticed that many of these cases referred to violence against women predominately by men and I was moved by the tragic resonances between then and now in the city of Glasgow which still has a disturbingly high rate of domestic violence. Reading through each article in more depth than my previous encounter, I took an interpretative approach paying attention to the language used to describe the people and places involved in the incidents. I started to notice the repeated patterns of dismissive language and lack of details given to the victims of crime, and the sensationalist details given to the violence itself. I began to connect to different feminist studies on historical crime and violence to help support my approach, taking inspiration from Hallie Rubenhold's study *The Five* (2019) which explores the lives (not deaths) of the five women killed by Jack the Ripper, and attempts to give agency to the women beyond their experiences of violence. I was keen to consider the personhood of these individuals and to remember that they were much more than what was being presented in these sources.

In doing such intensive work with the scrapbook and becoming immersed in stories of violence, I became increasingly aware of the ethical responsibilities I had to the material and to myself. Engaging with difficult material requires self-care and it is important to be mindful of your own limits and support needs. A particular article stood out to me that detailed the attempted suicide of a young woman called Jane Morton in Glasgow. Jane had been holding her baby as she jumped into the River Clyde near Nelson's Monument, and I was instantly moved and curious about what had driven her to such a desperate act. I noticed the name of the Humane Society where Jane and her baby had been taken after being rescued from the river and realised that it was a place that I walked past regularly on my way home from work. I decided to undertake a site visit to the spot and to consider the landscape in an embodied way, colliding historical and contemporary worlds

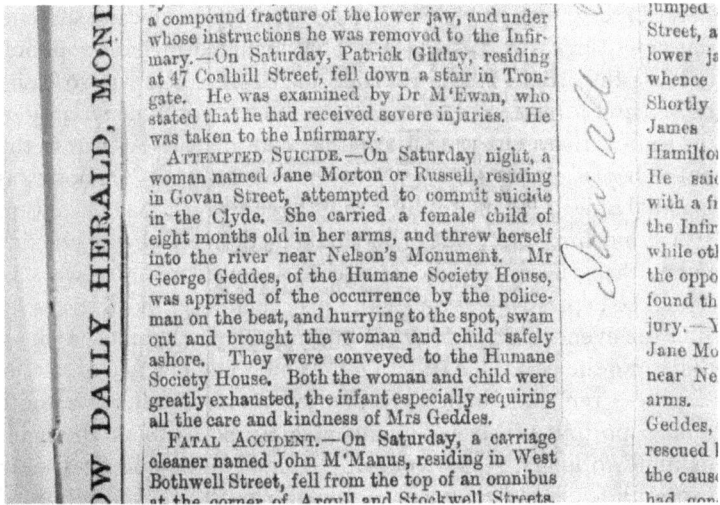

a compound fracture of the lower jaw, and under whose instructions he was removed to the Infirmary.—On Saturday, Patrick Gilday, residing at 47 Coalhill Street, fell down a stair in Trongate. He was examined by Dr M'Ewan, who stated that he had received severe injuries. He was taken to the Infirmary.

ATTEMPTED SUICIDE.—On Saturday night, a woman named Jane Morton or Russell, residing in Govan Street, attempted to commit suicide in the Clyde. She carried a female child of eight months old in her arms, and threw herself into the river near Nelson's Monument. Mr George Geddes, of the Humane Society House, was apprised of the occurrence by the policeman on the beat, and hurrying to the spot, swam out and brought the woman and child safely ashore. They were conveyed to the Humane Society House. Both the woman and child were greatly exhausted, the infant especially requiring all the care and kindness of Mrs Geddes.

FATAL ACCIDENT.—On Saturday, a carriage cleaner named John M'Manus, residing in West Bothwell Street, fell from the top of an omnibus at the corner of Argyll and Stockwell Streets.

Figure 5.4 Medical Scrapbook entry.

Source: RCPSG 10/9/10A.

(Figure 5.4). My fieldwork notebook recounts my emotional reflections on the landscape:

> The water is so still and calm today. in the sunlight it is hard to imagine Jane's descent into the murky depths below. I watch as people walk causally along the blue bridge, unaware and undisturbed by the events that happened here over a century ago. It makes me reflect on how places are momentarily ruptured by violence. Once a site of so much pain, it quickly repairs into something new. Yet the ripples of its suffering lingers. It feels sad sitting here now thinking of that night, I feel in some way connected to Jane and her story. I wonder what happened to her. Did she get help? Did her baby survive? Did the events of that night shape her future?
>
> (Research Diary Entry, June 2019)

Reflecting on the source itself I was struck by the physical smallness of the article in contrast to the enormity of what it conveyed.

Barely a scrap, the article would have taken up hardly any space in the newspaper that day and was only included in the scrapbook because the article above it related to Macewen. It was so easily missed and forgotten. This led me to reflect on the materiality of the sources themselves and to carefully consider these as part of the research process. Thinking about the journal and scrapbooks as material objects led me to think in different ways about Macewen, visualising him as a person undertaking police surgeon practice rather than simply a police surgeon. I considered the ways in which he expressively wrote about his experiences in the evenings after the events and carefully cut out newspaper clippings, sticking them into the pages. Considering the embodied practice of salvaging these remnants of his practice led me to construct a more human portrait of Macewen encouraging me to think about his own lifeworld. The experiences highlighted in these sources speak to the difficult and traumatising events that Macewen witnessed and affected his life in ways that remain untold, drawing to attention what new insights can be gained when exploring sources from different perspectives.

This example highlights that the process of working with historical sources is not a straightforward endeavour with multiple considerations and decisions made affecting the outcome of the research and the narratives that are crafted. It is also not a solitary practice with many different relationships forming between yourself and the source(s), the archive, archivist and the subjects themselves all which require critical consideration. In miniature this example encapsulates the core themes that we are covering in this chapter relating to exploring different kinds of sources, considering where sources can be located, how we can use sources in our research, and what are the ethical considerations that are intimately bound to our historical work. Also, as highlighted it can prove useful to keep a fieldnote diary while conducting your research, creating a further source for reflection. As researchers, we regularly note down detail when working with or extracting evidence, but it is also helpful to note your own reactions and emotions whilst conducting archival work. The following exercise provides a series of more specific prompts to guide your work with source material.

BOX 5.1 Exercise – Working with historical sources

Through engaging with the above example a range of questions relating to working with historical sources are raised for you to consider. We configure these here as a checklist of questions, many of which will be relevant to your own study no matter what your topic of investigation.

What historical materials can I use?

A significant challenge for students undertaking their first historical geography project is a concern over what sources are 'acceptable' or relevant for the topic they are keen to investigate. This uncertainty can create a barrier to starting historical work which is challenging for many to overcome. From the example above sketch out all of the sources that were used. What other sources would you have used to undertake this study? What alternative possibilities for sources do you feel could exist?

How do I find sources?

As discussed in Chapter 3 archives come in all shapes and forms and therefore locating archival materials can pose a challenge to the researcher starting out their processes of research. Thinking about where to look and furthermore how to access sources can seem overwhelming, even to the experienced researchers, as a great deal of work is often required before even engaging with the sources themselves. From the example above can you list the places where sources were found? Can you think of alternative places to look where other sources could have been discovered?

How do I work with historical sources?

Just like other methods of academic research it is important to understand how you are working with the sources that you have selected. Whilst there may be an assumption that you are simply 'reading' or 'looking' at the sources in front of you, this comes with a much wider set of interpretative skills that it is important to be aware of and be able to talk to. From this example can you list the different types of interpretation that are being discussed? What do you think these terms mean and what do you think are the differences between them?

Can you think of other interpretative or analytical frameworks that you might use with the same sources?

Should I connect sources?

Whilst some projects are entirely built around a single source this can be rare and instead a large proportion turn to connecting different sources to create a greater picture of their area of study. Archival sources can often act as important grounding work for further methods or can be supplementary to the knowledge gained in other ways, including interviews and field site visits. From the above example can you note how sources are being connected? What do you feel is the benefit of connecting sources?

How do I practically keep a record of my sources?

A number of practical considerations are required for working with sources that may seem small but can have a significant impact on our use of these sources in our research. Whilst the rise of digital equipment can be extremely helpful for undertaking archival research it is very important to think carefully about your use of this. For example, taking photographs of archival objects can be a helpful reference point but they are not the whole part of research. Remembering to keep track of reference numbers to properly cite your sources is really important. From the above example can you list the ways in which we kept track of the progress of our research? What mechanisms were used to record our research and how were they useful in our analysis?

Can I link theory to my sources?

As highlighted in Chapter 4 our theoretical positions can act as important shaping forces in how we undertake and write our research. Interpretation, note taking and coding our key thematics are all supported by the theoretical framework being used and become an important guide for our thinking and practice as we engage deeper with the sources we have located. From the example above can you locate the theoretical frameworks that we used for this research? How do you feel the research would be altered if we changed our theoretical approach?

What are the ethics that I should consider when working with my sources?

It is important to understand our own positionality and to notice the choices that we make that alters and shapes the research. Similarly to archives, as noted in Chapter 3, reflective practice is a crucial process for our working with historical sources, connecting us deeply into the ethics of undertaking historical research. Ethics in institutional settings is often restricted to work with human participants with those working with archival sources given only a supplementary form to complete. Whilst this appears bureaucratically enabling of the research process it often conveys the problematic sense that working with historical sources raises no ethical challenges that the researcher needs to consider. This could not be further from the reality as working with many historical sources raises deep ethical concerns that require critical reflection.

As recognised previously, archival work is an embodied and placed practice and further attention in historical geography is being paid to the ways in which these affect the process of the research itself. From the example above what do you feel are the key ethical considerations when working with these sources? How would you manage these ethical issues? What do you feel we can learn about our own work with the past through thinking about ethical issues?

WORKING WITH MEMORY – ORAL HISTORIES, PERSONAL OBJECTS AND OTHER HISTORICAL GEOGRAPHY METHODS

Whilst the example above was constrained to the archive as it remains, due to the date of the material considered, there are other subject matters that might lend themselves to a wider set of methods. In reflecting on my own practice (Griffin), I have noted how I have become increasingly drawn towards the potential for oral history to capture memories and experiences that the archive might not. This research has often worked alongside the material record, operating in a similar way to that described above whereby I have used the archive to understand the past. Yet more recently, opportunities have arisen to interview people about their past selves which has added a layer of insight into how I have understood the past. In this short section, I reflect upon this practice to encourage the possibilities for researching the past through oral histories. I also note some of the ways in which I have worked with this material and have begun to synthesise the abundance of material towards something which might be written up.

My initial research encounters within historical geography were largely archival. Although working with a different subject matter, labour histories and working class organising, I'd previously pursued archives associated with late nineteenth- and early twentieth-century history. My experience held much in common with that described by my co-author above, in that I looked to immerse myself into the lives of activists and workers during this period, following their campaigns and struggles to improve their conditions. About eight years ago, though, an opportunity emerged through conversations with trade unionists in North East England. They articulated a sense that their own past efforts to campaign and organise on issues of unemployment during the late 1970s and throughout the 1980s was somewhat hidden. As someone new to the region and looking for new research ideas, this opportunity excited me and was something I wanted to learn more about. It very quickly became clear that whilst some records did remain, much of the history associated with it was held within living memory. This required a different methodology, an approach to the past that activates and records memory. This methodology is known as oral history, a tradition that explores memories through interviewing.

With this new research opportunity emerging, I was conscious that the proposed methodology was a new one to me and I began to look for advice and guidance. Fortunately, there are several historical geographers who use oral history in their work and I found such scholarship extremely useful for understanding some key principles and approaches (see for example Hampton, 2022). I also began to have conversations with others using oral histories across geography and history departments. Equally, I was familiar with interviewing as a technique through both my teaching and other research practices. That said, there was clearly something unique around interviewing through memory. Put simply, rather than asking someone to respond to real world events in real time, I was proposing to ask participants about their life histories and events which, for some, occurred over 40 years ago.

Before I began my research, I knew that there was an ethical element to conducting the work and this was something to take very seriously. I began to draft information sheets and consent forms and looked to make these accessible in terms of my research purpose. To help with this, and all things oral history, I made considerable use of the Oral History Society (Britain and Northern Ireland) website which provides a series of resources and training for those wishing to undertake such research. It is crucial that your participants are fully aware of the purpose of the research and where their words might appear. For this reason, it is sometimes best practice to retain contact with your participants to check that they consent to being quoted in the way that you intend (although this is not always possible). What is similarly important, is that you establish whether they might be named or not in your research. For some social science research there are good reasons to anonymise participants but for historical geography there might be equally good reason to identify your participants. It is their stories, their life experiences, which you are looking to explore. Much of this depends on the subject matter and the wider ethical questions of conducting interviews, consent and anonymity have been well considered in human geography more broadly.

For oral histories, though, what is perhaps most exciting is the potential for our research to uncover new insights into the past. You might find a perspective that isn't found in the archive or a memory that indicates a new perspective into the past. Whilst memory is similarly haunted by absences and misremembering is always a possibility, as much as the archive is deemed partial and fragmented, how we remember still matters. In this regard, we consider oral history as only adding to historical geography, providing new perspectives to the archival record and having potential to be read alongside other historical traces.

My own work felt like a privileged position. I had time and resource to sit down with over 50 trade unionists and activists associated with unemployed activisms. They gave up their time, provided further evidence (sometimes through photos, objects or other personal archives – see Figure 5.5) and often signposted my research to others as a means to snowball the research. The interviews were rich in detail, around events and actions, as well as describing personalities. What also emerged was a sense of personal motivation and drive behind their involvement. In the example below, Kevin Flynn from North East England describes his belief that trade unions must have a role beyond the workplace, something was integral to the establishment of centres for unemployed workers:

> [Y]ou don't put your union card and your work boots at your locker at work, and when you come home you're no longer a trade unionist. You're a trade unionist when you're asleep, you're a trade unionist when you're off on holiday, you're a trade unionist at all times [...] So therefore the trade union should be fighting for you within your home, within your community, within your workplace, within every aspect of your life.

In preparing for these interviews, I would design an oral history schedule with a series of questions that I hoped to cover. Some participants were easily prompted with one or two simpler questions and a conversation would emerge, whilst others required a slightly more structured style to cover the subjects I wished to explore. The extract above emerged in an interview where the participant was quite comfortable talking through their past and only required the occasional prompt. Their interview offered much detail in terms of the who, what and where, but also added personal insights such as the extract highlighted above.

In this regard, oral histories tend to follow a semi-structured format, whereby you retain a sense of direction but remain open to tangents and participant led reflection. What was particularly interesting was how some participants would link their memories to particular objects or personal archives. Figure 5.5 shows a participant's t-shirt from the 1981 People's March for Jobs. The interviewee was keen for me to see it and it had clearly been carefully preserved. The t-shirt served as a key prompt in our interview, triggering memories and reflections. Such objects (think also of photos, films, newspapers, etc.) can prove useful reminders of past events and may prove useful prompts in an oral history interview. They also speak to the emotional meaning of materials from the past, which can sometimes be lost within an archival space which catalogues and orders the personal and intimate.

There is much more to be said about oral histories, and we would encourage you to make use of a wider set of resources if considering this as a methodology. The final reflection here, though, is around

Figure 5.5 Oral histories, personal archives and objects from the past.

Source: author's own.

how to handle the material you collect through the process. Interviews will require transcription and then you are met with the challenge of interpreting a vast amount of material and making sense of it. The nature of this task will differ depending on how you have conducted your research. If you have focused on a particular individual, for example through a biographical lens, then you might be looking for key events and reflections in their life, whilst for a project like that described above you might be working across a series of related participants. How you analyse this data presents a challenge.

My own approach was to analyse the interviews thematically via a coding exercise looking for trends and patterns across the interviews so to make some wider analytical reflections. Some of these are returned to in Chapter 6 where we talk about writing with historical geography and synthesising your 'pool' of data into something that can be articulated within piece of writing. This is also where your theoretical approach is useful as it might shape the focus of your analysis. For me, I knew that my particular interest was in labour geographies, and the practices of solidarity and resistance within unemployed communities. Analysis is time consuming and requires a lot of note-taking. There are technological and software options that can help with this, but most importantly it is spending time with your data to best understand it.

As already noted, oral histories perhaps work best when used in combination with other sources and materials. Sometimes participants might struggle to recall exact details (particularly the longer ago they were). It can be difficult to remember dates, names and sites, whereas emotions, feelings and memories are perhaps easier to recall. The latter are crucial for our storytelling, and whilst the former can be recalled (particularly around significant moments in people's lives) there is sometimes value in triangulating your evidence. Perhaps you can complement the oral history record with an account from the time. This isn't always possible, but in my own research I was able to find newspapers, trade union reports, photographs and even a documentary film from 1978 that corroborated and extended the oral histories mentioned above. This was particularly fulfilling as I was then able to share some of this extended data with a group of my interview participants. Such an exercise made the research feel worthwhile in more ways than one. It included bringing participants together, reuniting old friends, and my research felt more of a collaborative endeavour

SUGGESTED READING

Withers, C.W.J., Domosh, M. and Heffernan, M. (eds.) (2021) *The SAGE handbook of historical geography*. London: Sage. Especially Parts VIII and IX.

Millard, C. and Wallis, J. (eds.) (2022) *Sources in the history of psychiatry, from 1800 to the present*. Routledge Guides to Using Historical Sources. London: Routledge.

McGregor, R. and McGeachan, C. (2023) Undetected medical histories: William Macewen as Police Surgeon. *Scottish Archives*, 28.

Gagen, E., Lorimer, H., and Vasudevan, A. (eds.) (2007). *Practicing the archive: Reflections on methodology and practice in historical geography* (Historical Geography Research Series). Royal Geographical Society.

CONCLUSIONS

This chapter has used two research case studies from the authors to prompt a series of questions and considerations relating to your own use of historical sources in research. It has demonstrated the importance of paying reflexive attention to practice and how we work with sources to form our research. In doing so we have sought to offer a series of prompts to consider for your own engagement with historical sources. There is an impossibility to creating a chapter that charts out all the ways in which we can use sources, because just as each source is unique so is every historical geographer, and these individualities matter in the doing of our research. Whether you are working with documents, objects, people, landscapes, film or anything else, we have argued for the importance of reflecting on your own practice and for considering how this shapes the stories that you create. Using the police surgeon example we have drawn attention to the collaborative nature of working with sources and the importance of respecting the knowledges of others in our investigations. We have demonstrated how working with theory is important in shaping the directions of our practice and turned to consider ethics as not only a care for the people, places and worlds we are researching, but a crucial consideration for ourselves as practitioners.

Oral histories were also introduced here as an approach used by historical geographers to explore the recent past through memory. The approach can be especially rewarding and can provide new insights into how we understand the past. There are clearly limits here too, in terms of the reach of oral histories. Although increasingly we find oral histories appearing in archives too leading us to be able to use the interviews conducted by others to consider more personal insights and tales from the past. Memory remains crucial then for how we might uncover particular pasts and potentially reach some of the more hidden histories previously introduced.

A key message across both methods, and the multiple forms of data introduced, is the need for care in conducting your research (whether with materials or participants) and the potential to triangulate your findings. We encourage a detective like approach to the tracing of connections between sources and recognise how theory might also shape our analysis of that data, in a similar way to the theoretical steers introduced in Chapter 4. A subsequent challenge is turning these encounters with the past into a written output, and it is to this task that we now turn by considering how experiences like those shared above are translated to writing.

REFERENCES

Hampton, R. (2022) 'Towards an agenda for oral history and geography: (Re)locating emotion in family narratives of domestic abuse in 1970s East Kilbride', *Area*, 54(3), pp. 468–475.

Laing, R.D. (1965) *The divided self: An existential study in sanity and madness.* London: Penguin Books.

RCPSG 10/9/12 GB 250 10/9/12, Private Journal of Surgical Cases, 1872 – 1875, Sir William Macewen, (1848–1924), surgeon.

RCPSG 10/9/10A GB 250 10/9/10A, Medical Scrapbook, 1872 – 1874, Sir William Macewen, (1848–1924), surgeon.

Rubenhold, H. (2009) *The Five: The untold lives of the women killed by Jack the Ripper.* London: Doubleday.

6

WRITING HISTORICAL GEOGRAPHIES

INTRODUCTION

We're nearing the home stretch. So far, we hope that you've established an historical geography research interest, considered theoretical ideas that are linked to your topic and found sources to help you to explore that particular past. Following this, we hope you've spent time reflecting on the material you have found and began to analyse this. Whilst these stages have been addressed sequentially, we recognise that the reality of doing historical geography is largely an iterative process. You are constantly refining your approach, revisiting your position and developing your argument. The stages introduced overlap with one another and sometimes you might need to take a step back before you can move forward. This is completely normal. As such, your writing might not necessarily appear as the end point of your journey. You might find it helpful to write at different stages. At the very least, you're likely to be building up quite detailed notes as your research progresses. That said, writing remains a challenge for the historical geographer. How do we translate our engagements with the past into a well-articulated argument? How do we piece together fragments of the past to tell stories and connect with wider debates? This chapter looks to respond to this prompt by offering some advice around writing historical geography.

The chapter is split into two sections. These can be best summarised as firstly, the practicalities of writing pasts, and secondly a reflection on more creative writing styles within historical geography. The first section engages with advice around structure, presentation and some hints and tips around writing historical geographies.

DOI: 10.4324/9781003483588-6

The second, foregrounds more stylistic approaches of differing forms of writing within historical geography. Here, we note some historical geography modes of writing that have encouraged greater creativity and innovation in their approach. So, whilst the first section might seem to identify some elements of good practice and some suggestions for structure, the second section aims to encourage you to feel less tied to a rigid set of rules and to inspire you to find your own style. Writing is difficult and we must all find our own way. Writing with the past is no different. We are faced with a challenge of doing justice to past lives whilst also striving to tell wider stories or to engage with an audience beyond the subject matter of our study. We also all have our own writing styles and strategies. The authors of this book write in different ways, and we would not want to discourage you from exploring your own creative ideas with writing. Instead, we look to offer some advice by drawing upon our own experiences and reflections on writing within historical geography and human geography more broadly.

In what follows, we look to give some hints and tips around how to work with your material and how to write this up. The style and format will differ. A shorter essay is clearly more concise than a dissertation. Some writing might require sub-headings to structure your argument, whilst longer form writing might require chapters or clearer dividing lines and more regular signposting. Similarly, a blog post requires a different tone to an academic assignment. Yet, there are some principles and approaches which might benefit you. Read this chapter with a critical eye and borrow what fits with your intentions and ignore what might feel less appropriate. The chapter is primarily aimed towards academic writing and is structured across the two sections. The first section considers the transition from empirical material to writing on the page and considers some strategies for getting started. It then offers some hints and tips around including 'data' within your writing and how you might go about offering analytical insights. Following this slightly drier starting point, the next section offers some insights into more creative and innovative forms of writing, drawing primarily upon the work of cultural-historical geographers.

GETTING STARTED – FROM ANALYSIS TO WRITING

Dydia DeLyser (2009, p. 341) notes that the act of writing can be considered as 'a way of thinking, and a way of thinking through our research' and this assertion provides a helpful starting point for our comments on writing historical geography. Her argument is an important one for what follows. We recognise here that writing is difficult. The empty page staring back at you can be a daunting prospect. Yet, DeLyser's claims might offer some insights that motivate us to give it a go. She encourages writers to take on the blank page and jot down some thoughts and reflections. Her claim is that in writing we are also doing much of the analytical work required for understanding of research topics. It is with this premise in mind that we provide a few prompts and ideas for writing historical geography.

We recognise some of the particularities of writing with the past. In doing so, we offer some suggestions which might act as a guide to help with your writing. None of our suggestions are intended to provide rules or limits for your writing process and as we proceed, we will encourage more creative approaches to writing. Yet, we also recognise that some prompts and suggestions can also help move the writing process along. As much as anything here, our intention is to remove some of the barriers to writing. So, find a nice writing spot, identify somewhere that you work best, and look to focus on your writing task for an allocated period of time.

In the act of getting started we recognise some of the challenges this might pose. It is highly unlikely that you will leave the archive and feel ready to start writing immediately. You might have some tentative ideas or elements that you know you want to write about but there is still some way to go in terms of writing up your study. If you do have some early thoughts about your writing then make a note of these, often your instincts might lead you somewhere. But in terms of starting the writing process, there are a few elements to reflect upon. A starting point might be to revisit your notes and reflections from the archive (see Chapter 5). Revisiting these will familiarise yourself with your archival or oral history experience. Whatever your approach to qualitative data analysis, it is highly likely that you will have established some tentative themes or areas of interest within your research. As we switch to writing, we might now begin to consider how to order these thoughts, select best examples, and to shape your argument in relation to related works.

Before beginning your writing, you must try and understand the research subject as best as possible. This means understanding the archives, objects and/or oral histories you have considered but also the wider context within which they sit. Your reader needs to understand the framing of your material before you dive into some analytical and conceptual reflection. This means contextualising the materials and offering some wider details that help to frame your specific case study. This will likely require some engagement with secondary sources. These might include other scholarship on your topic. Can you identify key dates, events and individuals that will be integral to your discussion? You might not be able to establish all of this from your primary research (e.g. archival work and oral histories) but you can draw upon a wider range of sources to establish the context for your analysis. For example, if your work is analysing an asylum space in the nineteenth century, then you might want to give some information about the site location, when it was established, and how it fits with regional and national policy at the time. This information might be found within and beyond the archive, and some context might be shaped through reference to secondary sources.

Once you have established some context for your work, the second task is to establish your best examples to use in the discussion. Best examples can normally be described in one of two ways. First, in your analysis you might have established an emerging theme which is evident across your empirical study. Your task then, is to provide some evidence that reflects this wider trend within your research. This might be a particularly poignant or evocative quote, or an image that captures much of your wider description. In selecting this example, you are recognising that you cannot do justice to the whole archive and must select materials that best evidence your wider engagement. In contrast to this, your best example might be considered an outlier or an anomaly. This second approach is more aligned with the experiential dimension of researching the past and follows more of a researcher's instinct, than the more systematic thematic approach. Here, you might have discovered an item, quote or experience that you consider significant. Perhaps there is a story to be told that has not been previously shared. This sort of best example is equally relevant and useful but might be used and written about in different ways. Rather than reflecting a wider pattern or trend, the evidence (in the form of quote, image, object, etc.) is presented as of interest in its own right, perhaps as an anomaly that goes against the grain or simply as a distinctive story, which is considered worthy of analytical attention.

Generally, most historical geography work will have a combination of these two forms of evidence. So, look to be both analytical and instinctive in your approach to evidence selection. Our advice would be to have a 'pool' of evidence ready for when you come to write. It is highly likely that you will have too much evidence to fully utilise in your writing, but remember that this is a strong position to be in. Having these readily available will really help your writing and can assist you when you look to make a claim. Some form of data management will be needed here and Chapter 5 recognised some of the different ways in which historical geographers have ordered their archival reflections. We encourage you to use the method that works best for you and recognise the increasing use of technology to do so. Most importantly, whatever your method of storing notes and evidence, you will require easy access to your evidence as it will be required in shaping your writing. We will highlight how this evidence might be used in more detail later.

Once you have established your context and potential analytical themes, your next task is to shape the overall approach of your writing. Remember these tasks are not made in sequential order but instead give an indication of the key elements of writing historical geography. Indeed, it is highly likely that you will already have considered possible literature and theoretical insights before conducting your research, and in the shaping of your research questions (see Chapter 4). In order to frame your work, and thread through an analytical approach, you must establish a structure of writing that links back to existing work and looks to extend these in new locations and in varying ways. In this regard, your writing should look to build the theoretical focus by bringing some literature in conversation with your study. A useful starting point for this is to consider the approach your study is utilising and the key themes that attach most closely with the literature. In this regard, the analytical work with the 'data' should be considered as connected to the theoretical positioning explored in the literature review. As noted throughout the book, and specifically in Chapter 4, historical geography is particularly distinctive for its focus on theory in revisiting the past.

Finally, you might also wish to reflect methodologically on your work. This element of your writing might be of varying length, depending on the space that you have. In some instances, you might only be able to briefly acknowledge the sources used to develop your historical geography writing, whereas in other circumstances there might be more scope to reflect on the nature of your methodology, as well as to acknowledge what went well and if there were any limitations in conducting your research. Either way, some methodological reflection is useful and we have stressed this in Chapters 3 and 5. Your methodology is an opportunity to reflect on the nature of your engagement with the past (perhaps by reflecting on the archive, or the practice of oral history) and also to directly link this to your experience of engaging with sources. In recent years, there have been several methodological reflections presented by historical geographers, which might prove useful to consider when developing your own methodology (e.g. see Hampton, 2022; Hodder, 2017).

To help with these four tasks, you might want to visualise your own writing. Sometimes it can be difficult to see how the paragraph you are writing fits within the whole piece you are developing. And this challenge becomes more and more apparent the longer your writing becomes. Visualising your work can help summarise the key elements you wish to include. In Figure 6.1 we provide an example of this, which informed a recent publication by one of the authors (see Griffin, 2024). The visualisation was useful for displaying some of the key elements that were to be included in the written output. Viewing these elements together serves as a useful reminder of the key elements that should be included in the writing, and some of the connections that will need to be threaded through your account.

For example, your discussion of analysis and results should be conscious of the theoretical underpinnings of your work. So, in the writing of the paper on the People's March for Jobs in 1981, the author was constantly shifting between the oral histories collected and the theoretical underpinning of the research. Equally, the author was aware of some of the key evidence to include (e.g. quotes and images) as well as some of the thematic areas to be considered (e.g. solidarity infrastructures, experiences and imaginaries and tensions). Similarly, your work should always look to contextualise the discussion and being conscious of this can be a useful reminder to not assume your reader is fully aware of the times and places you are writing about. Again, in reference to Figure 6.1, this required the author to acknowledge the particularities of 1980s Britain, and some of the wider forces which were shaping the experiences found (e.g. rising unemployment and emergent neoliberalism). Similarly, there was some methodological particularities that required acknowledgement in the write up. In this section, look to consider your own methodology rather than general comments about the archive. For the paper mentioned here, this required some acknowledgement of the archives being specifically aligned with working class histories as well as some comment on the shaping of oral histories and the role of key gatekeepers in recruitment.

In Figure 6.1, we being to see an emerging structure and set of themes that might be covered. Your challenge is to similarly establish the writing focus for your study. This might require a few attempts at the exercise (Box 6.1). The example (Box 6.2) was refined regularly

BOX 6.1 Exercise – Mind-map your writing

Planning your work can really help with your writing, and visualising this in some format can provide a useful tool and reference for your writing. Before beginning your writing, you might find it useful to produce a mind-map in a style similar to Figure 6.1. This can be done quite easily with pen and paper, or if you prefer you can produce it electronically. In producing the visualisation, you should look to include the following:

1. **Title** – a working title is fine for now; you might experiment with this further down the line.
2. **Context** – consider what context is required for the reader to understand your study. Key dates, events, individuals all require some level of introduction and you may wish to cite some secondary sources in doing so.
3. **Theory** – some indication of the academic literature you consider your topic to connect with. Where possible, look to include literature within human geography but also be open to extending your reading list with influences from elsewhere.
4. **Methodology** – indicate your key methodology and associated debates, whilst also identifying your sources and how they were used.
5. **Material/themes** – this is an opportunity for you to establish what material you will include in your write up. This will be considerably less than the data you collected. You should look to include best examples of wide themes and trends, as well as any materials that stood out that you as particularly meaningful/impactful.

This will not be the final version of what is included in your writing, but the exercise begins to give you an overview of the piece you are writing. This can then be useful for creating the threads and connections as required in academic writing.

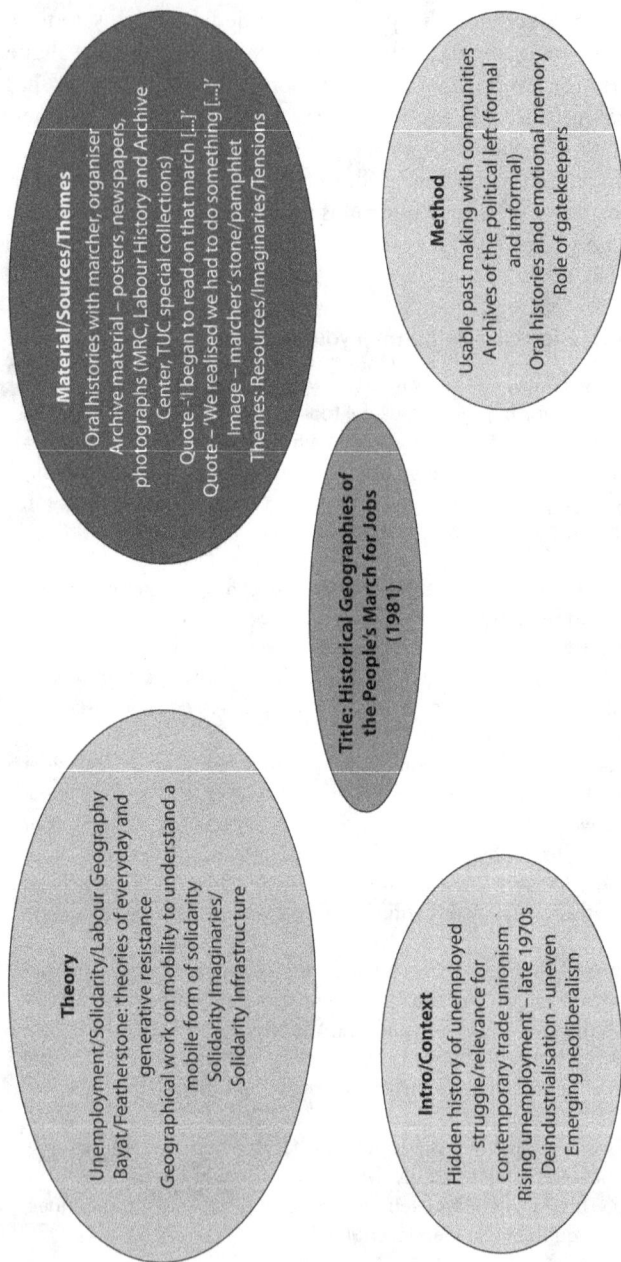

Figure 6.1 Mind-mapping historical geographies – an example from our research.

Source: author's own.

over time, through constant back and forth, mostly between the literature and the results gathered. This allows the refining of approach and crucially the shaping of argument. In the example given, it became increasingly clear that the evidence found was speaking back to the geographies of solidarity literature and that the evidence was indicative of the resources required to build solidarity as well as the more intangible elements that sustained activist involvement. This simple premise became a key touching point for the paper throughout and was noted and signposted regularly. This sort of overview is necessary for all writing as it helps give a sense of purpose and direction. This then continued to develop through the building of evidence, the widening of the literature review and the eventual establishment of three key areas for detailed discussion. Moving beyond this, the chapter now considers some key principles for the writing of historical geography. It briefly considers some key sections of your writing and some practical advice for doing so. Following this, the chapter moves towards a more critical and creative engagement with writing as found within historical geography.

WRITING WITH HISTORICAL DATA – PRACTICALITIES

Once you come to write-up your work, you are likely to consider questions of structure and how best to order your words on the page. Again, this task is not an easy one and your approach might be shaped by the particularity of the assignment. Generally, though, there are some key elements which should be included in your work and these map on to the visualisation notes provided above. The extent of each will be shaped by your word limits and any constraints placed upon your work. So, the advice below is offered as a guide and as the final section explores, do consider more creative ways in which you might include these components but perhaps with more creative and engaging structures and styles. To start with, we indicate a suggested structure for your writing and some of the elements you might wish to include in each.

- **Introduction** – An opportunity to draw your reader in and state your intentions, including an indication of your structure. This might also include some context and justification for what is to follow, allowing your reader to step inside the history you are so familiar with. Some detail on the who, what, and where of your study might be worth including here. Where relevant, you might also want to give an indication of your research aim and/or questions.

- **Literature review** – A section of your writing might want to consider the academic framing for your work. This is an opportunity to indicate your broader approach (where relevant) and to also situate your work in relation to related studies. This might blend together the theoretical framework of your work (e.g. feminist historical geographies) as well as the more specific ideas you wish to explore (e.g. ideas of the home and domestic labour).

- **Methodology** – Where possible, you should look to include a section that considers your sources and the nature of collecting your data for use in your study. This section should blend together the specific (perhaps the archives used, or the participants recruited for oral histories) alongside the more general methodological comments (around the nature of archives, working with fragments, or the nature of oral history as exploring memory). As noted above, there is an opportunity here to connect your own approach with the existing literature on researching the past.

- **Results/discussion** – This is the opportunity to revisit the past in detail and with analysis (more on this below). As noted previously, it is highly likely that you will have some themes and arguments that you wish to explore and unpack in your results. Perhaps these are thematically structured, and some sub-headings will help group together your findings. Crucially, this section should look to set up your key claims and support these with evidence. Where possible, these claims should then speak back to the literature as a means of comparison with previous work (either subject specific or theoretically linked). It is sometimes useful to think about the results section as sitting in conversation with the literature review (more on this below).

- **Conclusions** – A final section should look to tie some of the previous sections together. This is your opportunity to repeat some key arguments, to remind the reader of where you have taken them and perhaps to suggest some future openings. Do not ignore this section. At times as a writer it can feel less significant, but as a reader it is a really important bookend to your argument.

Working with this structure, you should look to personalise and adapt the sections to fit with your own project. Generally, we would encourage you to be specific with your sub-headings and to offer these as a guide through your analysis. So perhaps avoid the more generic placeholders in Figure 6.1 (particularly 'literature review' and 'results') and instead look to indicate sub-headings as pertinent to your study. Before engaging with more creative forms of expression within historical geography, we now briefly turn to some of the specific writing challenges faced by the historical geographer and some of the strategies you might use to overcome these. Thus far, we have looked to provide some prompts and guides for your writing. These are mostly aimed as strategies for structuring your work and ensuring you are covering some of the distinctive features of a historical geography approach. The actual writing of these sections has yet to be considered. So, our next consideration is to briefly reflect on the act of writing with evidence. We turn to focus on this specific element because we assume that other elements of your writing are considered elsewhere. For example, your writing of a literature review is likely to share some similarities with other forms of essay writing, and your methodology is more of a reflective account of your activities and situating these in relation to literature on the archive and/or oral histories.

So here, we wish to turn to how our writing can use evidence and the importance of analysis. There are some elements you might be particularly mindful of the need to:

- Signpost/introduce the relevance of your evidence.
- Contextualise as much as required, whilst recognising that this context might be provided elsewhere.
- Present your evidence accurately and format appropriately. Select best examples to reflect wider themes. Include sources for any archival material.
- Where possible, look to present multiple forms of evidence to build an argument.
- Analyse, analyse, analyse. Do not assume the reader understands the relevance of your evidence. Take time to unpack and explain why the material has been selected and how it contributes to your argument.
- To help with this, you should compare your findings with literature. Does your work make a similar claim to somebody else, if so indicate that. Alternatively, you might find your results contrasts with others, this is your opportunity to identify this. At the same

item, not all findings sit as neatly as this and you may wish to think about how your results offer nuance, complexity and detail to existing debates.

These are key components that might help your writing with historical geography data take shape. Figure 6.1 suggests that your literature review and results sections might be considered as sitting in conversation with each other. To help with this, we provide two extended passages from our writing where we look to utilise some of these principles. These are taken from two longer papers and have links to content already covered in the book. Box 6.2 provides an example from the paper associated with the mind-map in Figure 6.1 and utilises some archival evidence associated with the 1981 People's March for Jobs. Box 6.3 shows the framing of a quote previously presented in an exercise for Chapter 2. The content here is less relevant than the approach evident in the writing. This is intended to provide an example of how some of the principles indicated above might be included in your writing.

BOX 6.2 Example from Griffin (2024)

Commenting on the march's arrival into London, Livingstone suggested that 'their presence at County Hall transformed the building' with 'a confidence that these marches radiate.' His reflections also noted the potential for infrastructures to be generative of imagined solidarities and atmospheres, which might in turn inform political action:

> Having those marchers sleeping in there using that building changed the whole climate and ever since then it's been open to trade unions, black groups, women's groups through London and I think something will happen this time. It's hard to say what it is, a sort of confidence that these marchers radiate sticks in the building, humanises the building in a way.
>
> (Ken Livingstone interviewed in 1983 by People's March for Jobs marcher. Labour History and Archive Centre, Manchester. "Interviews from People's March for Jobs 1983". People's March for Jobs files. Uncatalogued)

Here the material structures are viewed as integral to the sustenance of a movement, both in terms of the provision of nourishment and for building endurance and strength, but there is also a sense that the people occupying the space have the potential to remake and reimagine the environment. His comments reflected a reimaging of a political space and the transformative potential of solidarity as expressed through the act of marching (Featherstone, 2012). Crucially, it was the multifaceted unemployed at the centre of this action, articulating a message demanding jobs. Including them here, offers a reappraisal of unemployed people as active agents in shaping an alternative dialogue, as well as a commentary on the spatial politics of working-class resistance and solidarity.

BOX 6.3 Example from McGeachan (2018)

Recognising the complexity of emotional terrains within prison, Crewe et al. (2014, p. 67) discuss the marginal spaces where normal rules of prison society can be partially suspended and a broader emotional register enabled, for example the display of warmth and tenderness. In the case of the Barlinnie Special Unit, the entire space was designed to act along these marginal principles, in this wider emotional context, attempting to produce an 'emotional microclimate' (Crewe et al., 2014, p. 67) where vulnerabilities were exposed and kindness could be shared. Boyle (1977, p. 229) recounts one of these small yet significant acts in his memoirs:

> I was then asked by a screw if I would come round and sort out my personal property with him. I went, and while we opened the parcels containing old clothes he did something that to him was so natural but to me was something that had never been done before. He turned to me and handed me a pair of scissors and asked me to cut open some of them. He then went about his business. I was absolutely stunned. That was the first thing that made me begin to feel human again. It was the completely natural way that it was done. This simple gesture made me think. In my other world, the penal system in general, such a thing would never happen.

This 'mind-blowing' moment for Boyle, after all '[h]ere I was, still awaiting trial for six attempted murders of prison staff and being given a weapon by one of their colleagues' (Boyle, 1984, p. 11), relates to the significance of these marginal spaces to the remit of the Unit. However, these are also often mediated acts where boundaries and relationships are deliberately tested. In the above example, the individual who controversially handed over the scissors to Boyle was Ken Murray, an experienced prison officer and advocate for penal reform. As a principal investigator of the Special Unit concept, Murray was keen for it to succeed and knew the significance of his actions (Wilson, 2007). Murray first met Boyle in Inverness and was keen to gain his trust in the new space of the Unit. He was acutely aware that giving Boyle access to scissors was a gamble, but it paid off. A marginal space was therefore created where emotional bonds were made and a platform created for a new type of relationship to build that highlights in miniature the complex synergies between care and control in these experimental spaces.

The two examples show good practice in several ways. They both draw upon a quote as evidence to support their wider claims. These quotes are introduced and situated in relation to the wider argument of their writing. In example 1 (Box 6.2), there is a note that the evidence is in relation to the arrival of an unemployed workers march into London, as well as a sense that there is an interest in solidarity, as both imagined and infrastructural. In example 2 (Box 6.3), there is an indication of an engagement with prison space, as a site of emotional interest, as well as the set-up for a quote from somebody who experienced this space. Both examples use an extended quotation to evidence their claim. Evidence like this can take many forms, including photographs, field notes, oral history quotes and tables/figures, but detailed evidence is crucial to develop depth in your argument. Whilst single examples are presented here, your longer writing should build an argument by aggregating evidence.

What is also key here is that they are appropriately referenced and where necessary footnotes to archival sources should be included (see example 1). The extended quotes are also separated from the rest of the paragraph. It is generally good practice to do this if your evidence runs over three lines so to avoid confusion in differentiating your own claims from the quoted evidence. Following the quotes, each example provides some unpacking of the evidence so to stress the key points and to link back to the associated literature. Example 1 highlights some analysis of the evidence, drawing attention to the role of support and space in shaping the march, before linking with geographical work on solidarity and working-class politics. Example 2 adds additional evidence to support the quote before then expanding the analysis in terms of understanding the Special Unit within which the experiences were felt. In contrast to example 1, there is more detail and context provided here and at times this may be necessary, but crucially the analysis still returns to the geographical themes around emotions and relations within carceral space.

It should be evident then, that there is no simple formula, and our advice is that good writing takes time and often several drafts and rewriting. To help with this, it is generally useful to find willing readers for your work. Both of our examples benefitted significantly from peer support in their development. Writing can be an isolating task and sometimes it can be difficult to see the strengths and any weaknesses in your work. A second pair of eyes can often quickly identify any problems in your work and indicate any confusing points. Such an exercise can speed the process up of fine-tuning your work and strengthening your argument. Before moving on to more creative forms of writing then, we ask that you consider Exercise 6.4 at a time that works for you in the preparation of your writing.

Thus far, our discussion of writing has been fairly formulaic. We've given some indication of the elements which *might* be expected of you as a historical geographer. Yet, in doing so, our intention is not for every historical geographer to write the same. Nor do we want to create a writing straight-jacket of rules and structures that you must conform to. Instead, these are hints and tips which might help shape your own writing style. In doing so, we also want to stress the power of creativity when writing and the scope for you to shape your own writing style, to tell historical geography stories and to engage different audiences. With this in mind, the chapter now turns to writing forms as found within historical geography, with an emphasis falling upon more creative writing and modes of expression that have pushed us to think more critically about the forms of presentation within the sub-discipline.

BOX 6.4 Exercise – Drafts, feedback and peer-review

Writing historical geography is difficult and can lead to us falling into some common pitfalls. These can include using overly long and unedited quotes from sources or wider literature, overwriting, and balancing speculation with evidence. Sometimes we become so close to our research topic that we forget some of the basics of (re)telling pasts and this is where reviewing and editing our work becomes of paramount importance. Before making your submission, we suggest that you find at least one friendly peer to review your work. They needn't be academically aligned with you but should be able to offer some insight on your work. In reading your work, you might ask them to consider:

1. Did you understand the past I was looking at? Were there any details missing?
2. Did my evidence make sense?
3. Were the sub-headings clear?
4. Was my writing clear in making key points? Could you follow my argument?
5. Was it clear where my evidence was taken from?

Depending on who your reviewer is, they might be able to offer detailed feedback on each of these elements or perhaps might be best placed to respond simply to question 1. Perhaps you have a course friend who might look at your work to offer greater insight into the theoretical position of your work, but often the main purpose of a second opinion is to simply establish that your writing makes sense! You can also consider expanding your writing skills and set of critical friends by attending writing retreats and creating peer spaces of support that will help build your confidence and abilities.

WRITING HISTORICAL GEOGRAPHIES OF PEOPLE AND PLACE

The first section of this chapter has introduced a number of practical considerations for writing your own work and developing your writing style. We recognise the challenges that are associated with writing, particularly in relation to the past, and have sought to provide some hints and tips to help you to get started on your writing journey. However, often it is helpful to gain insight and inspiration into the ways that others have considered and developed their writing practices, and this chapter now turns to these wider terrains by providing insight into some of the ways historical geographers have explored writing. Attention is given to the writing of place and lives as a way of exploring innovations in writing across historical geography, particularly giving insight into creative approaches. Critical considerations to writing the past are also noted as a reminder to consider carefully the power relations embedded in writing. We hope that this section provides a space for reflection on writing, offering inspiration for your own work and igniting new questions for you to consider both before, during and after the writing begins.

WRITING LIVES

Interest in writing within historical geography extends across multiple terrains highlighting the specificities of places and environments and capturing details of people and encounters. One area that illuminates varying aspects of these approaches to writing is the resurgence of attention to life-writing and biography within historical geography, described sometimes as geographical biography (McGeachan, 2021) or bio-geographies (Patchett, 2019). Whilst specific terminology differs and connects to particular traditions of writing and scholarly activity, the interest in telling the lives of others continues to generate great curiosity with many historical geographers devising innovative and creative ways to story lives at varying scales. We can make connections back to our discussions in Chapter 4 of Robert Wellesley Cole here and think about the different ways we configured his life through varying theoretical frameworks, changing what parts of his life were fore-fronted and those that were marginalised in the writing process.

Hayden Lorimer's (2003) notion of telling 'small stories' has been particularly generative within historical-cultural geography for developing new ways of creatively exploring and writing everyday subjects and experiences. This turn to the small and the everyday moves away from traditional biographical approaches that have often deliberately prioritised grand narratives of powerful and known lives, such as royal figures, politicians and celebrities, and instead focuses on narrating 'ordinary social lives' and their intimate geographical relations. This move has offered an important challenge to those writing the histories of geography, turning attention away from (re-)telling the grand narratives of 'heroic' figures within the discipline to writing about a wider diversity of lives and experiences that influence geography's making (Maddrell, 2009). This has been particularly evident in the growing sets of conversations between historical geography and the history of geography that through geo-biographical approaches are enabling the emergence of a wider set of non-Western actors, concepts and institutions to come to the fore (Ferretti, 2019).

As described throughout the previous chapters, historical geography is often working with remnants and what can be traced through different archives and processes. In the writing of a life, lives or life-worlds this attention often turns to thinking about what remains and what can be found in official archives, riffled through in home spaces, stumbled upon in attics or meticulously searched for in the landscape. In many ways the writing of lives turns to consider the practices involved in the creation of them, leading to many historical geographers critically reflecting upon the entangled connections between their practice and their writing:

> Historical geographers have spent, and continue to spend, time and creative energies investigating presences in life-writing and biography, drawing upon diverse materials, from documents to memories, artefacts to landscapes, detailing their historical usefulness, cryptic inaccuracies, beautiful distinctiveness and wider connections.
>
> (McGeachan, Forsyth and Hasty, 2012, p. 169)

As McGeachan, Forsyth and Hasty (2012) notes this is often a creative venture and requires historical geographers to move into more exploratory domains. This includes writing narratives that reflect upon unknowing and uncertainty, sharing vulnerabilities, and cojoining the lives of the researcher and the subject in intricate ways. This is often powerfully revealed through the inclusion of autobiography and autobiographical reflections, pulling together the geographies of a life. For example, Terri-Anne White (2004) in her explorations of Theodore and Brina reconstructs the myths and facts of the course of her own family life over five generations of a female line, as it runs along and across established social histories of the settlement of western Australia. White deliberately deploys creative writing in order to attempt to break down the boundaries between conventional genres of history, autobiography, memoir and fiction. In recalling family stories of Perth from the mid-nineteenth century to the present White reflects on her own archival practice revealing the difficulties inherent in writing lives. She reflects:

> I have become a collector of shards. Shards of memory, things passed down: told to me at the end of this long line of telling. I want to catch these shards, these half-lit, often, paste jewels. I don't know how authentic they are, does it even matter? For me it doesn't matter. I am making anew, building something from the remains. Wanting to honour the fleeting; the fragment, fractured histories and stories. Not passed down, but dredged up.
> (White, 2004, p. 520)

White incorporates elements of absence into her narratives which becomes a crucial tool for narrating her biographies, stating explicitly that it is the very gaps and silences that are driving her storytelling.

For a number of historical geographers, the creative potential of biography and life-writing offers an exciting avenue for opening up new connections between people, experiences and places. As noted, the lack of material evidence for researching lives leads not only to creative forms of practice but also narration. Imaginative life-writing is one form that has recently gained momentum in historical-cultural geography and is often mobilised through the form of the essay. For example, Fraser MacDonald's (2014) narrative essay detailing the story of the Scottish archaeologist Erskine Beveridge and his family demonstrates the power of storytelling to shape life-worlds and their afterlives. Through a focus on Beveridge's house situated on the Hebridean island of North Uist, MacDonald evocatively brings the historical geographies of the Beveridge family and their home into present conversations relating to land ownership and troubled familial relations. Individuals from the family, such as George Beveridge, haunt the overall narrative, and his death marks a pivotal point in the essay which seeks to convey a move away from lamenting ruination and instead to attune to the awakened ghosts with the 'unremarkable sorrows' (MacDonald, 2014, p. 487). Whilst these creative interventions play with form and structure and find ways of telling that sit within the realms of absence and creative reconstruction, the boundaries between fiction and non-fiction, slippery as they may be, are seemingly still being maintained. MacDonald (2014, p. 479) explicitly states that he is not writing fiction and that '[t]he provenance of this story matters to its telling,' setting a hazy boundary between lives we imagine and those we fictitiously create.

The slippery line between imaginative biography and fiction creates a malleable space for some historical geographers to work and write within. A resurgence of interest in considering counterfactuals has arisen, particularly in relation to exploring interactions between human and environmental change. David Gilbert and David Lambert (2010) turn to consider worlds that might have been, in connection with the historical geographies of the sea. Utilising Doreen Massey's focus on notions of 'possibility' and 'chance,' Gilbert and Lambert (2010) look to draw attention to counterfactual agendas within historical geography, raising a set of questions relating to the counterfactual method and counterfactual imagination. These include:

What are the explicit and implicit historical geographies in existing counter-factual writings and analyses?
How might historical geographers think, work and write counterfactually in distinctive ways?
What are the historical geographies of counterfactual analyses and writing?
What political, ethical and emotional demands do counterfactuals make?
(Gilbert and Lambert, 2010, pp. 249–251)

Throughout this questioning lies a curiosity in the power for expanding the counterfactual method in historical geography providing innovative inquiries into 'what might have been' and inspiring increased creative attention to imagining alternative lives and worlds. This interest and experimentation with creative writing as outlined throughout this section speaks to the wider 'creative turn' (Hawkins, 2018) within geography that has diversified the styles and forms of writing used to explore key concepts such as place, space, landscape and environment. Tim Cresswell (2024), for example, reflects upon his dual position as poet and academic geographer noting that there is much that unites the two, and advocates for a more entangled approach that can expand the way we view and think about worlds and those who inhabit them.

BOX 6.5 Exercise – Writing counterfactual historical geographies

Counterfactual historical geographies inspire us to creatively imagine new stories of worlds that might have been. In this exercise you are encouraged to develop new ways of writing that capture alternative ways of considering climate change and environmental historical geographies.

This exercise relates to the Katherine Leah Pace's (2023) article 'Shifting terrains of risk: A history of natural hazards and displacement in three historic black communities of Central Austin, Texas' that can be found in the *Journal of Historical Geography*. In this work Pace traces three case studies of historic black communities in Texas to consider the interplay between natural hazards and the hazards of displacement.

Firstly, read through the article and focus on one of the three case studies that you would like to explore counterfactually. Think about the key details of the communities and their histories that are being raised. Take note of the impacts of the hazards on the lives and landscapes.

Secondly, pick a particular element of the story that you would like to develop. Does it relate to issues of race, population, housing, rivers, disease, land, displacement, etc.?

Imagine the varying ways that your chosen element could have been different and develop a new version of the story.

Reflect upon the process of imagining worlds that could have been. How does this change or alter your understanding of the histories in the case study? Does it help you to connect with different elements more emotionally? How does it help to draw attention to injustices?

These experiments with counterfactual writing are designed to be exploratory and creative ventures that help you to understand the historical worlds you are writing in more depth and to critically consider the power of stories to shape our future engagement with the past.

An interest in life-writing and biography stems for many historical geographers from the multiplicity of narratives and stories that can emerge and the variety of lives that can emerge. As Norman Denzin (1989, p. 81) notes:

Lives and their experiences are represented in stories. They are like pictures that have been painted over, and, when paint is being

scraped over an old picture, something new becomes visible …
There is no truth in the painting of a life, only multiple images
and traces of what has been, what could have been, and what
now is.

This interest in the multiplicity of lives and their stories is also
reflected in the array of geographies that can be revealed. Lives have
complex geographies and many historical geographers are utilising
the tools of biography and life-writing to carve open new ways of
understanding these complex spatialities. Stephen Legg has demonstrated a number of ways in which historical geographers can compile
different biographical traditions to reveal the lives of British reformers
and further critically explore the spaces of colonialism. For Legg
(2008) utilising different approaches to life writing – chronological,
analytical and genealogical – work to uncover particular parts of an
individual's life that be generative for reconsidering spatial politics
and practices. As further attention falls to considering decolonial and
anti-colonial perspectives across historical geography ways of config-
uring narratives of lives continues to diversify. Questions regarding
'whose lives are worth living? Whose lives are worth writing about?
Whose lives are worth remembering?' (Scarparo, 2005, p. xi) become
increasingly pertinent to the sub-field, raising vital questions about
the exclusions within writing practices and posing critical questions
about the future use of biography and life-writing as a tool to represent worlds and experiences.

BOX 6.6 Exercise – Geographical biography

Geographical biographies can be described as stories of people,
objects, places and worlds that move across time and space, and act
as a tool to inspire us to understand in more depth the lived geographies of, often, the most marginalised of people.

In this exercise we are going to be looking at materials in a make-do
archive relating to the life of Janella Lewis (Jan). Jan lived in Glasgow,
Scotland with her partner, Arthur, until moving to a care home in the
last year of her life after Arthur's death. Jan died in 2024 when she
was 83. Jan's brother Raymond, and sister-in-law Moira, sought out
anyone who could take her large collection of artwork. Jan had created

art all of her life and used art to represent her experiences of the world, particularly her relationships with family and imaginative worlds of her life as it could have been. Jan had spent large periods of life experiencing mental ill-health and was institutionalised many times at a local psychiatric hospital in Glasgow. She experienced significant trauma during her 20s as a psychiatric patient, leading to a mistrust of individuals and medical authority. As Jan lived in a council house her brother only had two weeks to clear out the property and was desperate to find the hundreds of pieces of art a new home otherwise they would have to be thrown away. The artwork was collected by the author (McGeachan) on the proviso that it would be used to find ways to try to tell Jan's story.

Task 1 – Think like an archivist

As noted in Chapter 3, archivists have a power to shape our ideas and access to historical materials in varied ways. For this exercise you are required to put your archivist skills to the test by creating a catalogue description for each of Jan's pieces. Think carefully about what you want to present about each piece and how this might guide the researcher in certain ways. Each description should be no longer than 50 words and contain details relating specifically to the piece. Think about your word choice and how you are writing the description, reminding yourself that your writing has power over how others may interpret these pieces and Janella's world.

As highlighted in this chapter, geographers think about life geographies when tracing the lives of others that is different from conventional biography. For this exercise imagine that you are writing a research article about Jan and creating her geographical biography for the *Journal of Historical Geography*. Write down a list of questions and details you would like to know about her life. Consider the methods you may have to use to find out these details and what archives you may have to use. Try to come up with at least eight questions.

This exercise highlights some of the complexities and ethical challenges relating to geographical biography and gives you insight into how you may wish to develop your own investigations in writing lives. It is also designed to broaden your thinking relating to archives and how these can be seen to be constructed in peculiar and make-do ways (Figures 6.2–6.4).

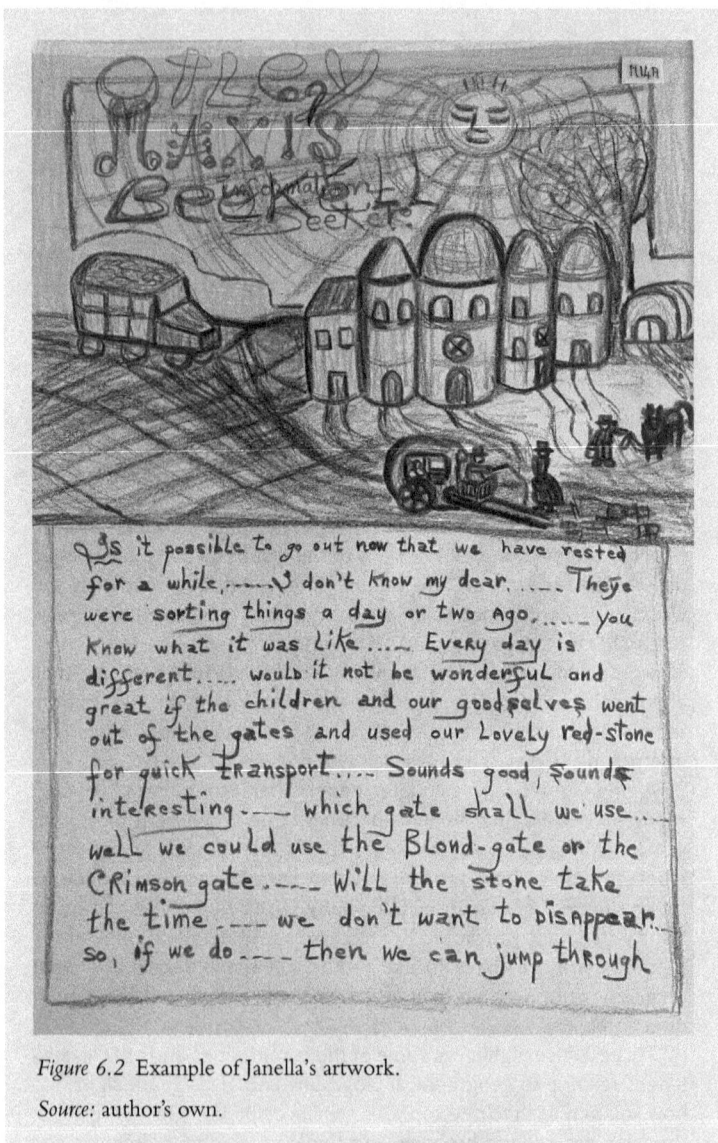

Figure 6.2 Example of Janella's artwork.

Source: author's own.

Figure 6.3 Example of Janella's artwork.
Source: author's own.

Figure 6.4 Example of Janella's artwork.
Source: author's own.

WRITING WORLDS

In a special issue of the *Journal of Historical Geography*, Steve Daniels and Catherine Nash chart the close connections between the art of geography and biography, stating that 'life histories are also, to coin a phrase, life geographies' (2004, p. 450). Concentrating on the lexicon of the lifepath, they draw to attention how an increasing attempt within historical geography has been made to situate individual lives within their widely worldly landscapes. This culminates with the before described desire to turn towards the small in the writing of lives, and to consider how we write our worldly narratives to gain insight into alternative, hidden and marginalised experiences. One particular strand of this centres on geographical writing about place as a 'lived phenomenon' (Lorimer, 2019), as referred to in Chapter 2. Questions of style, form, language and convention all become debated and trialled as historical geographers look for new ways to write about place, leading to a wide range of expressions becoming visible in place-writing. In his writing of pet cemeteries, Lorimer explores:

> But when it comes to dead pets, the language of love slips the leash, runs unmuzzled. So the pet cemetery is full of ... gush. Appreciation is voiced for devotion, obedience, rascality, warmth, trust, sacrifice, affection, bravery, nobility, honour. And simply: for companionship. Parting words are chipped out in Doric, corner dialect of Scotland's north-east, so that fingertips can lovingly trace the lettering. Hewn from granite, language is unmistakably a material thing.
>
> (Lorimer, 2019, p. 337)

For many historical geographers writing about geo-bio-graphical aspects of place connections are made to aspects of 'materiality' and 'the material' to recognise the co-presence of the 'non-human.' Lorimer (2005) stresses that the 'rematerialisation' of human geography calls for a recognition of the way that materials and social worlds intertwine in all manner of combinations. A key aspect of this for historical geography becomes the attention to 'the rethinking of the object' as a means of (re-)discovering the materiality of everyday life and the power this has to creatively shape our engagement (and writing) of our worlds.

As noted in previous chapters, an innovative example of this kind of work and writing is DeSilvey's (2007) work on the Art and Archive. In this piece DeSilvey challenges practices of inventory, collection and curatorial practice through pieces with peculiar qualities and so-called waste things which tie into the broader reflections in historical geography on research methods that are receptive to 'small stories' and overlooked histories. DeSilvey (2007, p. 900) notes:

> Working down the margin between art and archive, where the past comes into being through its creative recuperation, I found a different kind of memory at work. This was not Nora's nostalgic living memory of peasant ritual and extinct sensibilities, but a lived memory that arose out of a creative engagement with material remnants in place.

This process of creative recuperation becomes pertinent to a range of historical geographers who attempt to write through, and with, material matter in their excavations of the past. Slatter (2019) advocates for increased attention to exploring the wide range of material matter in historical geography, in the forms of objects, things, ephemera, buildings, urban and rural landscapes, man-made structures, the animate and inanimate and the human and the non-human, leading to the attention to provide alternative, and often more personal, insights into well-established historical stories.

However, whilst many historical geographers have written about the small stories of life geographies others have utilised the method of biography to chart different aspects of global historical geographies. Attention to the historical geographies of modernity has led historical geography to take seriously interconnected historical geographies of modernity. For Nash (1999, p. 22):

> Historical geographies of modernity map complex and specific interconnections between places and between different processes. But thinking about interconnected historical geographies of modernity also means paying attention to how these connections between places are understood.

Thinking about the ways in which these interconnections are understood leads to a number of important questions arising regarding who is experiencing them and how are they being storied across space and time? Ogborn (1998, p. 2) argues that 'the literature on modernity is full, paradoxically, of both ambiguity and totalisation' and therefore refining our approach to narrating modernity becomes vital. Contextual and historical geographies of modernity, Ogborn (1998) argues, allow for a multiplicity of moderni*ties* to be revealed while retaining a sense of large-scale and far-reaching changes.

Ogborn, in his book *Global Lives* (2008), demonstrates one way of writing about modernities through attention to lives that shape and were shaped by these global processes. Sketching out the remit of this work, he stresses:

> Parts of the world that were previously disconnected became connected in novel ways; important reconfigurations of empires and trade routes were established that operated beyond the confines of nation-states; the lives of many people were increasingly shaped by the decisions made by others who live far away in new centres of power and control; cultures and landscapes were reworked as people, ideas and material objects were transported and recombined elsewhere in unprecedented ways.
>
> (Ogborn, 2008, p. 1)

Key to this work is the storying of globalisation through fragmentary narratives of lives and their connections to places, processes, ideas and objects. Paying particular attention to the transformative, Ogborn brings to life biographical portraits often hidden in the sweeping narratives of modernity. One such figure that features in these accounts, and that has become of interest to historical geographers, is that of the pirate. Pirates have captured the imagination of writers for centuries, highlighting their violent and mystical appeal in equal measure. For historical geography writing into pirates focuses on tracing their histories to show (often violent) economic and political processes, but also to draw attention the range of complex maritime stories about people, place and practice that are often missed when focusing so completely on the land (Hasty, 2011).

To highlight these interweaving narratives we can turn back to Ogborn's (2008) writing to consider how he has storied the life of female pirates in his accounts of global lives. Ogborn describes the world as being turned upside down by the eighteenth century, so much so he notes that women were turning pirate. The definition of pirate, '*hostis humani generis*: the enemies of all humanity' (Ogborn, 2008, p. 170), pushes at the boundaries of a feminine notion of violence and situates the role of pirate in a more masculine domain leading to a strangeness being associated with women turning pirate. Ogborn shares the biographical story of Anne Bonny to consider the changing worldly relations captured through maritime stories. Anne Bonny was born near Cork in Ireland in 1698 and was likely to have been the illegitimate daughter of the lawyer and eventual successful plantation owner, William Cormac. Anne moved to South Carolina and married a poor sailor called James Bonny in 1718. Dismissed by her father for marrying James, she moved to the Bahamas to find work. It was here that she met buccaneer 'Calico Jack' Rackman and deserted her husband to start a new life at sea with Rackman, Anne had been raised as a boy by her father and when she went to sea she returned to wearing male clothing in order to disguise herself on the ship. However, Anne certainly didn't hide herself from duties on board the ship and took part in violent activities relating to piracy in the eighteenth century.

It is believed that on board Anne met another woman, Mary Read, who was also disguised as a man. They fell in love and began a relationship. When the ship was finally captured, all of the pirates were sentenced to death and hanged, except Anne and Mary, who had been reprieved on the grounds that they were both pregnant with Rackman's babies. In writing about the lives of Anne, Ogborn (2008) notes that the stories revealed of hidden gender and secret sexualities may simply be just that; stories, that have been created and circulated in order to scare and thrill people on the land and strengthen the belief in the 'otherness' of the pirates. This attention to the worldly stories of pirates forefronts the importance of moving our writing across scales to trace the most intricate of geographies amongst powerful global forces. It also highlights the multiple nature of the stories that we are working with as historical geographers. The writing of Anne's story can highlight varying aspects associated with her life including gender, sexuality, power and the law, to name but a few, and can be useful in understanding the wider implications of these aspects for our understandings of maritime worlds and how they are created and occupied. Yet the ways that we tell Anne's story have significant implications for how we know and understand her and her world. Ogborn's insight into how he has conveyed Anne's life as a potential story, one that may not be true, reminds us that as historical researchers we are often building our own writing on stories that have gone before and the rewriting of these creates new stories that are layered across space and time. Understanding our writing as often *re*writing leads us to be more critically aware of the limits of what we can know, and to be more reflective of the ways we write our worldly stories.

WRITING WITH CARE AND CAREFUL WRITING

This section of the chapter has highlighted the potential our writing has for capturing and conveying new insights into the past. Yet it also raises a range of tensions that exist for us as we try to find ways to write about people, worlds and events of the past. The many examples of historical geography writing we have used throughout this book highlight the political nature of writing, demonstrating the power words have to capture worlds that have been lost, marginalised, obliterated or forgotten. Yet they also draw to attention to the limits of words for capturing experiences, introducing us to moments where words fail to articulate the depth of feelings and embodied connections with human and non-human experiencing (McGeachan and Philo, 2014). Writing therefore becomes one way in which we can express the historical geographies we research but we must remain open to considering what lies beyond words and the alternative ways that these can be conveyed.

A focus on writing brings to our attention issues of power and the need to be caring and careful with our words. Writing is not a neutral act and is embedded with choices that we make which reflects different aspects of power and privilege, and our own positionalities. Take for example the work of Trevor Barnes and Christian Abrahamsson (2015) in their research into the tangled complicities and moral struggles of Karl and Albrecht Haushofer. In their work, the authors slowly unfold Karl and Albrecht's lives in order to highlight the multiple struggles of individuals caught up within this deadly regime of the Nazi state. In doing so they seek to demonstrate the complex relationship between Nazism and academic labour (labour of geographers), and the wider web of familial relations that becomes entangled into complicity. Writing about tragic aspects of their death, Barnes and Abrahamsson (2015, p. 73) note:

> Karl Haushofer's fate was as tragic as his son's. A little less than a year after Albrecht's murder, Karl Haushofer and his wife of nearly fifty years crept out late at night from their large farm house in Hartschimmelhof, Southern Bavaria. They went down a 'dirt road' to a 'secluded hollow' on their estate. Around 11 pm they drank a cordial laced with arsenic, with Martha finishing the job by hanging herself from a tree branch. Karl was too enfeebled to do the same, dying 'sprawled, face down'. Heinz found the corpses the next day. He had gone to the house looking for them, and in their bedroom he discovered 'letters of farewell. on the pillow, together with a neatly drawn diagram showing where the bodies would be found'. Karl's suicide note ended: 'I want to be forgotten and forgotten.'

A tension arises here regarding the wishes of Karl, who explicitly denotes his desire to be forgotten, and the aims of the historical geography work itself. Barnes and Abrahamsson acknowledge this tension directly as they reveal that have deliberately gone against the suicidal wishes of Karl by forcing his life to be remembered in ways he sought it not to be, and are clear about their reasons for negating Karl's pleas for the catharsis produced from knowing about the difficult moral struggles and tragic tangled complicity faced in the lives revealed. They also note that they believe doing so can 'deepen, enrich and complicate understanding of the historical experience, without making motives of the complicity appear either simply lurid or base' (Barnes and Abrahamsson, 2015, p. 73).

This example highlights the complex decision making we are faced with in our writing about people and worlds that are no longer able to give permission. For many of us working with historical materials we are told by university ethics committees that our lack of *living* human participants requires us to complete fewer forms and paperwork. However, as Elizabeth Gagen (2021) in her reflections on exhibiting sensitive historical photographs argues, raising the awkward and thorny questions of ethics in historical geography is crucial if we are to strive for a caring and careful approach to researching the past. When thinking about our own lives we may feel uncomfortable about details of ourselves being revealed in the future and the lack of control we may have over this. It may feel upsetting to know that someone is sharing information about our private experiences in ways that may contradict how we want these stories to be told. As writers of the past, we have a responsibility to consider these tensions and explore these in our work. For example, a pertinent question that has arisen within historical geographical writing around lives is when should we leave the dead alone? This is not an easy question to grapple with and returns us back to acknowledging issues of power that haunt all aspects of historical work. Making the decision to write about a life, or to leave it alone, creates a dynamic of power that is important to recognise. Calls for more collaborative and participatory approaches to historical geography (Thompson, 2024) illuminate the challenges associated with these power dynamics and particularly 'writing for' the lives of others.

Considering how we might collaborate in our historical writing endeavours provides interesting and exciting routeways to challenging some of these issues of power. For example, including experts by experience in whatever field you researching into the work, such as people with lived experience on your topic, and sharing your writing drafts or writing your work *with* them (if appropriate) can be one way to diversify the power dynamic. However, as Hayden Lorimer (2014) in his excavations into family histories conveys, this is no straightforward process and often requires careful negotiation. Yet the potential collaborative working has for extending our writing practices and creating new critical and productive conversations around power is tremendous in scope and worth considering in the development of our own writing.

SUGGESTED READING

DeLyser, D. (2009) 'Writing qualitative geography,' in DeLyser, D., Herbert, S., Aitken, S., Crang, M. and McDowell, L. (eds.) *The SAGE handbook of qualitative geography*. London: SAGE, pp. 341–358.

Peters, K. (2017) *Your human geography dissertation: Designing, doing, delivering*. London: SAGE.

Rather than listing a long set of general readings about writing, we instead encourage you to consider the writing that is most relevant for you. Find an article that is closely related to your own study – either empirically or conceptually. Consider how the article is written, how evidence is presented, and how analysis is threaded through. Paying attention to writing style, as well as writing content, can be particularly helpful for shaping your own approach. It can inspire and encourage you to try out new forms and styles, and to consider what writing works best for the audience you want to reach.

CONCLUSIONS

This chapter has introduced some writing principles alongside some more creative approaches to shaping your output. These have primarily focused upon academic writing, but we also recognise that other outputs (media, blogs, teaching resources, etc.) might take an alternative form or that a more accessible writing style might be necessary for different audiences. That said, many of the points highlighted here are provided as a guide to help develop your own writing style. As has been regularly stressed, these are not rules or limits for how you might revisit the past. Instead, they are ideas for you to work with. Equally, some of these suggestions are not distinctive to historical geography and some of the points around writing and analysis are likely transferable to contemporary human geography too. That said, we have attempted to stress some of the particularities of writing historical geographies, and how these might be most helpful in shaping your work.

We have also stressed how writing is a form of expression that can be more creative and innovative in how we work with the past. We have scope to craft and edit, shape and mould our expression so to (re-)tell pasts in a way that communicates meaning through past lives, events and places. Such writing can be playful and imaginative and should not be constrained by a sense of rules or limits. Instead, consider how the act of writing shapes your own understanding whilst influencing others too. This might well take several iterations to get right, but you should feel empowered to shape your own narrative, in your own words, and through your own use of evidence.

In concluding this chapter then, some key principles can be summarised for writing within historical geography can be described as the following:

- Historical geography writing requires contextualising. Take time to indicate where, when and how your evidence emerged. If you are focussing on particular sites, individual lives or events then give contextual detail for them too. Do not assume prior knowledge from your audience.
- Historical geography writing requires evidence. Take time to select best examples and consider presentation styles. Might images help? How might quotes be used? This is a crucial layer of preparation before beginning your writing. Keep a close note of your sources, for example archive reference numbers, as these should be included in your write-up (generally as footnotes).
- Historical geography is theoretically informed. Consider the concepts that are most relevant to your study and look to return to these when analysing your findings.
- Historical geography writing can be creative. The final section took a much wider look at how we might write historical geographies. You should feel able to express yourself creative and to include more creative forms of evidence and analysis.

REFERENCES

Barnes, T.J. and Abrahamsson, C. (2015) 'Tangled complicities and moral struggles: The Haushofers, father and son, and the spaces of Nazi geopolitics', *Journal of Historical Geography*, 47, pp. 64–73.

Cresswell, T. (2024) 'Afterword: Geography and the creative writer,' in Alexander, N. and Cooper, D. (eds.) *The Routledge handbook of literary geographies*. London: Routledge, pp. 419–428.

Crewe, B., Warr, J., Bennett, P., and Smith, A. (2014) 'The emotional geography of prison life', *Theoretical Criminology*, 18, pp. 56–74.

Daniels, S. and Nash, C. (2004) 'Lifepaths: Geography and biography', *Journal of Historical Geography*, 30(3), pp. 449–458.

DeLyser, D. (2009) 'Writing qualitative geography', in DeLyser, D., Herbert, S., Aitken, S., Crang, M. and McDowell, L. (eds.) *The SAGE handbook of qualitative geography*. London: Sage, pp. 341–358.

Denzin, N.K. (1989) *Interpretative biography*. London: SAGE.

DeSilvey, C. (2007) 'Art and archive: Memory-work on a Montana homestead', *Journal of Historical Geography*, 33(4), pp. 878–900.

Featherstone, D. (2012) *Solidarity: Hidden histories and geographies of internationalism*. London: Zed Books.

Ferretti, F. (2019) 'Rediscovering other geographical traditions', *Geography Compass*, 13(3), p. e12421.

Gagen, E. (2021) 'Facing madness: The ethics of exhibiting sensitive historical photographs', *Journal of Historical Geography*, 71, pp. 39–50.

Gilbert, D. and Lambert, D. (2010) 'Counterfactual geographies: Worlds that might have been', *Journal of Historical Geography*, 36(3), pp. 245–252.

Griffin, P. (2024) 'Solidarity on the move: Imaginaries and infrastructures within the People's March for jobs', *Transactions of the Institute of British Geographers*, 49(3), p. e12637.

Hampton, R. (2022) 'Towards an agenda for oral history and geography: (Re)locating emotion in family narratives of domestic abuse in 1970s East Kilbride', *Area*, 54(3), pp. 468–475.

Hasty, W. (2011) 'Piracy and the production of knowledge in the travels of William Dampier, c.1679–1688', *Journal of Historical Geography*, 37(1), pp. 40–54.

Hawkins, H. (2018) 'Geography's creative (re)turn: Toward a critical framework', *Progress in Human Geography*, 43(6), pp. 963–984.

Hodder, J. (2017) 'On absence and abundance: Biography as method in archival research', *Area*, 49(4), pp. 452–459.

Legg, S. (2008) 'Ambivalent improvements: Biography, biopolitics, and colonial Delhi', *Environment and Planning A*, 40(1), pp. 37–56.

Lorimer, H. (2003) 'Telling small stories: Spaces of knowledge and the practice of geography', *Transactions of the Institute of British Geographers*, 28(2), pp. 197–217.

Lorimer, H. (2005) 'Cultural geography: The busyness of being 'more-than-representational'', *Cultural Geographies*, 29(1), pp. 83–94.

Lorimer, H. (2014) 'Homeland', *Cultural Geographies*, 21(4), pp. 583–604.

Lorimer, H. (2019) 'Dear departed: Writing the lifeworlds of place', *Transactions of the Institute of British Geographers*, 44(2), pp. 331–345.

MacDonald, F. (2014) 'The ruins of Erskine Beveridge', *Transactions of the Institute of British Geographers*, 39(4), pp. 477–489.

Maddrell, A. (2009) *Complex locations: Women's geographical work in the UK 1850–1970*. RGS-IBG Book Series. Wiley-Blackwell.

McGeachan, C. (2016) 'Historical geography II: Traces remain', *Progress in Human Geography*, 42(1), pp. 134–147.

McGeachan, C. (2018) ''A prison within a prison'? Examining the enfolding spatialities of care and control in the Barlinnie Special Unit', *Area*, 51(2), pp. 200–207.

McGeachan, C. (2021) 'Tracking traces of the art extraordinary collection', in Ellis, R., Kendal, S. and Taylor, S.J. (eds.) *Voices in the history of madness: Personal and professional perspectives on mental health and illness*. Series: Mental health in historical perspective. Cham: Palgrave Macmillan, pp. 219–236.

McGeachan, C., Forsyth, I. and Hasty, W. (2012) 'Certain subjects? Working with biography and life-writing in historical geography', *Historical Geography*, 40, pp. 169–185.

McGeachan, C. and Philo, C. (2014) 'Words', in Roger, L., Castree, N., Kitchin, R., Lawson, V., Paasi, A., Philo, C., Radcliffe, S., Roberts, S.M. and Withers, C.W.J. (eds.) *The Sage handbook of human geography*. London: SAGE, pp. 545–570.

Nash, C. (1999) 'Historical geographies of modernity', in Nash, C. and Graham, B.J. (eds.) *Modern historical geographies*. Michigan: Longman, pp. 13–42.

Ogborn, M. (1998) *Spaces of modernity: London's geographies 1680–1780*. New York: Guilford Press.

Ogborn, M. (2008) *Global lives: Britain and the world, 1550–1800*. Cambridge: Cambridge University Press.

Pace, K.L. (2023) 'Shifting terrains of risk: A history of natural hazards and displacement in three historic black communities of Central Austin, Texas', *Journal of Historical Geography*, 79, pp. 39–51.

Patchett, M. (2019) 'The biogeographies of the Blue Bird-of-Paradise: From sexual selection to sex and the city', *Journal of Social History*, 52(4), pp. 1061–1086.

Scarparo, S. (2005) *Elusive subjects: Biography as gendered metafiction*. Leicester: Troubador Publishing.

Slatter, R. (2019). 'Materialies and historical geographies: An introduction', *Area*, 51(1), pp. 2–6.

Thompson, L. (2024). 'Dancing in the archive: Bodily encounters, memory, and more-than-representational participatory historical geographies', *Area*, e12982.

White, T.A. (2004) 'Theodore and Brina: An exploration of myths and secrets of family life, 1851–1998', *Journal of Historical Geography*, 30, pp. 520–530.

7

FUTURE IMAGININGS IN HISTORICAL GEOGRAPHY

INTRODUCTION

As we reach the final part of our *Basics* introduction to historical geography, we wish to return to some key ideas to consider what we have learned and reimagined about our own engagements with the past. Chapter 1 of the book began with a short exercise where you were asked to consider a past of your own choosing. We start this chapter by asking you to return to that initial idea. It might be that you have actively pursued this project throughout the book and therefore identified links with some of the key ideas and tools presented. Equally, you might have moved away from that initial prompt and instead taken your interests in a new direction, perhaps inspired by the many ideas and works cited throughout the book. Either way, it is at this point that some further reflection is worthwhile. With this in mind, we begin the concluding chapter with a short exercise revisiting our initial prompts and questions. Our hope is that you now feel better placed to respond more critically to the questions and are more confident to frame your interests in historical geography terms.

This book has offered a range of insights into how you may respond to these questions and strengthen your engagement with historical geography. Chapter 1 began with a number of entry points for thinking through historical geography. It introduced the subdiscipline, highlighted key sources and identified a variety of changes in how historical geography has developed. The chapter concluded with references to contemporary events which are indicative of the continued relevance of the past in the present. We return to this in

DOI: 10.4324/9781003483588-7

BOX 7.1 Exercise – Revisiting your ideas as a historical geographer

The initial questions posed prompts that can be summarised as follows:

1. Consider a history of interest to you.
2. Where is this documented?
3. How is this history represented – are they dominant or hidden narratives?

We might now wish to extend these questions with some further prompts, now that historical geography has been introduced:

1. How might an exploration of this past be justified in the present? How might this past be considered usable?
2. How might the archives you used be understood as sites of power relations, collaborations, absences and presences?
3. How might you utilise a theoretical approach in your study?
4. How do you intend to tell the stories of these pasts?

some concluding remarks below. Chapter 2 illustrated the variety of research interests as found within historical geography. Crucially we looked to stress the role of space and place in shaping our approach to the past, identifying three scalar entry points for revisiting the past through a geographical lens.

Following these two chapters which surveyed the sub-discipline, we then turned specifically to investigating the archive and our practice as historical geographers. We indicated the archive as a different kind of place where aspects of the past can be traced but also noted the dynamics through which the archive is shaped and created. The chapter acknowledged the different forms archives might take, hinting to the diversity of sources that can be used and considered in our storying of the past. Finally, the chapter asked methodological questions, which are particular to the historical geographer, whilst also encouraging more analytical and critical engagements with archival material.

Chapter 4 moved away from the archive itself and towards the more abstract theoretical and conceptual tools which can be utilised within historical geography. We identified this as a key strength of the sub-discipline. The ability to link the specific detail of the past with wider, more transferable understandings is something to aim for in your work, whilst also acknowledging how our approach shapes the pasts we tell. Several examples were drawn upon in the chapter to identify how this might work in practice, with the life of Robert Wellesley Cole considered in depth to show how different approaches might illuminate different elements of his life. Chapter 5 extended this by providing a more practical set of insights into working with the past. We drew upon our own experiences of encountering archives to show how the past is collated, ordered and analysed in our own work. This process is unique to each researcher and each project but nonetheless some of the challenges are shared by historical geographers. This chapter looked to engage more closely with the realities, emotions and strategies for conducting research through the past. Our penultimate chapter, Chapter 6, then switched attention to writing historical geographies. The first part of the chapter acts as a guide to writing, from starting to consider the style and structure of your work, to considering the act of writing itself. The chapter then turned to widen our engagement with writing through demonstrating different ways in which historical geographers have written about lives and place at varying scales.

It is important to stress that the book has been constructed in a particular order that echoes different stages of the research process, but each stage is not necessarily sequential – you may find your route to the final historical geography output is more convoluted and complex than the simpler structure outlines in this book. It is not uncommon, for example, to return to the archive during the writing stage. It might be that you need to revisit a source, or you might have only paid passing attention to something that becomes increasingly significant as you move through your work. Similarly, your analysis will be a constant process, with your ideas and arguments continually evolving.

HISTORICAL GEOGRAPHIES AND HOPEFUL FUTURES

In writing this book we have been mindful of questions relating to the future of historical geography. Not every Geography Department in Higher Education will have a historical geography module, nor will every human geographer wish to explore the past. Indeed, some scholars working with past lives and events might not even consider themselves historical geographers, nor perhaps wish to do so. The sub-discipline has always been difficult to define in that regard, with a porosity that can be viewed as equally a strength and weakness. Yet, our reading for this book has revealed a world of historical geography that is vibrant and multifaceted. We don't claim to have definitive answers of where historical geography may be or might look like in the future. However, we share a hopefulness in the spirit of community that it produces, and this book has been an attempt to illuminate the exciting possibilities of forging a new generation of historical geographers. It is our belief that the past has never been more relevant, providing a key resource for understanding contemporary crises, challenges and injustices. Similarly, we wish to convey that there is often light to be found in the past, something more hopeful that can be grasped even in the darkest of histories. This hope drives us to continue to adapt our practices and continue to story the most forgotten, marginalised and unjust of pasts. We make this claim whilst recognising the limits of our own perspective. Our aim in writing this book, though, has been to provide a series of transferable ideas and skills that might be taken in new directions within different contexts. Put simply, we are advocates for the continuation of historical geography and the important work it does to critique, convey and consider the past in all of its complex manifestations.

Returning to the notion of a usable past we wish to use it as an entry point for thinking about possible future engagements with historical geography. As noted previously, the term usable past is mostly associated with the development of social history in the 1970s and 1980s and was a response and challenge to top-down, master narratives and foundational myths primarily surrounding nation building. It has entered into geography through these bottom-up roots and planted itself firmly within certain elements of historical geography. The usable past works as a conceptual framework to help us, as historical geographers, get to grips with the multiplicity of pasts by acknowledging that behind every version of the past are a set of interests in the present. Through this lens the past is often used to open new avenues of exploration in the present, to disrupt seemingly straightforward narratives and to strengthen contemporary ideas and movements.

If we take the Suffragettes as an example, we can see how this can be the case. Historical research into the suffragette movement is vast and can be utilised in the present to discuss and advance debates about women and their place in society. A recent illustration of this is in relation to the protests that took place in Ireland in 2022 over the right to have access to abortion. Ireland has a near-total ban on abortion, pushing thousands of women every year to travel abroad for a termination and others to break the law by taking abortion pills. Connecting these two issues is, of course, the demand for justice and equality for women but it also brings to the surface the importance of the body politic. Historical investigations into the bodies of the suffragettes on the street, in the courtroom, on rooftops, at the race-course, in prison, on the doctor's table, to name a few, can all be used in the present to showcase that women's bodies are still in many ways controlled and contained by the state and patriarchy (see McInerney, 2025). In connecting past protests to the present a wider argument about female emancipation and the fight for justice and equal rights for women comes into view (Moore, 2018). The arguments of women in Ireland no longer become a singular moment and instead become part of a longer trajectory of fighting against state violence and control. And so, a usable past can become a powerful connecting force across time and space.

The notion of a usable past has been discussed at length in historical geography through the lens of carceral geography. Highlighted earlier in this book, carceral geography broadly relates to the study of prisons and this incorporates physical prison spaces, the governance of society, criminal justice systems and the lived experiences of prison. Within this body of work Karen Morin and Dominique Moran are asking historical geography to take seriously and apply a usable past to the study of carceral space. From the outset they make it clear that:

> [T]here really is no point in studying the past unless there is something we can learn from it. The past must be made relevant, have purpose, and make a difference.
>
> (Morin and Moran, 2015, p. 1)

Attention to a usable past here demonstrates their desire for research in historical geography to bring about progressive social transformation and to find new ways forward for implementing prison reform. These are powerful ideas however, it is important to note that not everyone is convinced that a usable past is a useful one. Some critics hold the view that presentist accounts are invented to deliberately manipulate, distort or falsify certain accounts and to generate particular agendas. And in uncertain times this is something that we must keep forefront in our mind. Therefore, usable pasts must always by its very nature ask the questions usable by whom and for what end or purpose?

Whilst we acknowledge the difficulties and critiques of a usable past, we believe that it provides a powerful platform for considering future engagements with historical geographies. As Hitchcock (2013) conveys:

> History from below cannot awaken the dead. It cannot 'make whole what has been smashed'. But by placing the lives and agency of people most in danger of being forgotten in the centre of our regard, by filling the air with their stories, worries, loves, and tragedies, perhaps history from below can calm the storm blowing out of paradise, and give us a chance to rescue meaningful lives from the ever-growing pile of historical 'debris' and from the silences, forgetting, and revisions of modernity.

It leads us to consider the future potential of our research, both in and beyond academia, and connects us back to enlivening debates within the archive. Growing calls for participatory and emancipatory approaches to historical geography (Crawford, 2024) are advocating for more attention to be paid to progressive and liberatory research efforts (DeLyser, 2014) asking us to think more carefully and creatively about how our work can strengthen and advance real-world agendas in the present and beyond. In this regard, our work might not end with a mini-project, essay or dissertation; instead, our skills might find a place outside of the academic setting. Throughout this book we have generally remained focused on exploring the academic approach found within historical geography, but we have also raised the possibilities of collaborating with others within and beyond higher education.

Most prominently, we wish to stress the potential for working with archives, libraries and museums. There is tremendous scope here for further conversations relating to working-*with* others, and the historical geographer has great insight to offer. You might even consider writing a blog or donating your oral history interviews to a relevant archive. There is great potential in the world of social media that can act as an archive of the future and a site to disseminate our shared findings. Online worlds are increasingly where our experiences are likely to be documented (whether on social media or through electronic correspondence). These might be viewed as the diaries and letters of contemporary times. Similarly, resources such as Google Street View Archive (with data already dating back to 2007) are likely to reshape how we can research urban historical geographies in the future. Historical geographers are well placed to work with archivists on these questions of how best to archive the present for the future.

As a means of concluding we wish to give insight into the future of historical geographies through the visions and imaginations of

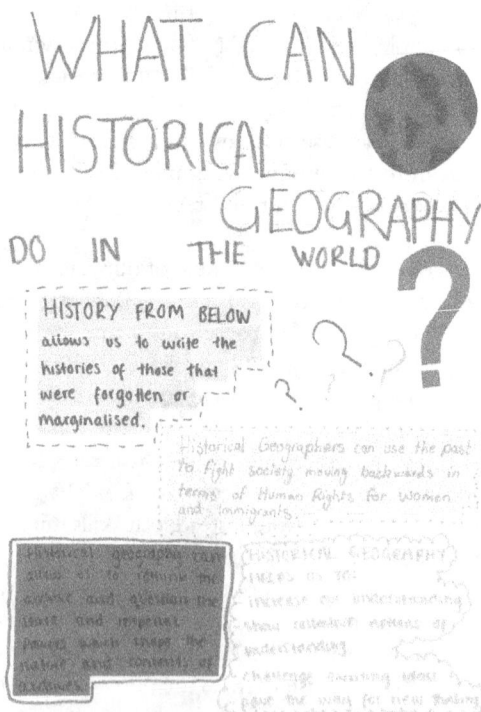

Figure 7.1 Example manifesto 1 from Historical Geographies Honours Course 2024, University of Glasgow.

Source: author's own.

up-and-coming historical geographers. In our Historical Geography teaching modules, we both ask our students to consider what they believe historical geography research can do in the world, encouraging them to reflect upon their own hopes for the future of historical geography. In the spirit of usable pasts, and our own belief in the importance of historical geography work for building more just futures, we asked students to create their own historical geography manifestos. We close this text with a compiled version that speaks across the different themes raised in our classes in the hope that it may encourage, inspire and motivate your own ambitions in historical geography (Figures 7.1–7.4).

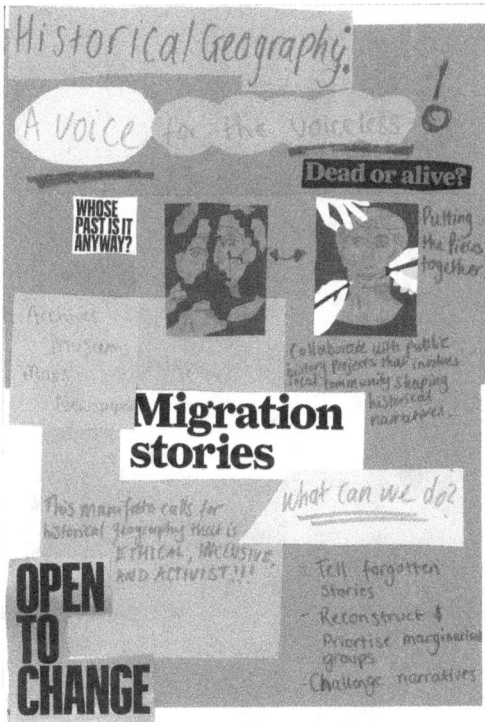

Figure 7.2 Example manifesto 2 from Historical Geographies Honours Course 2024, University of Glasgow.

Source: author's own.

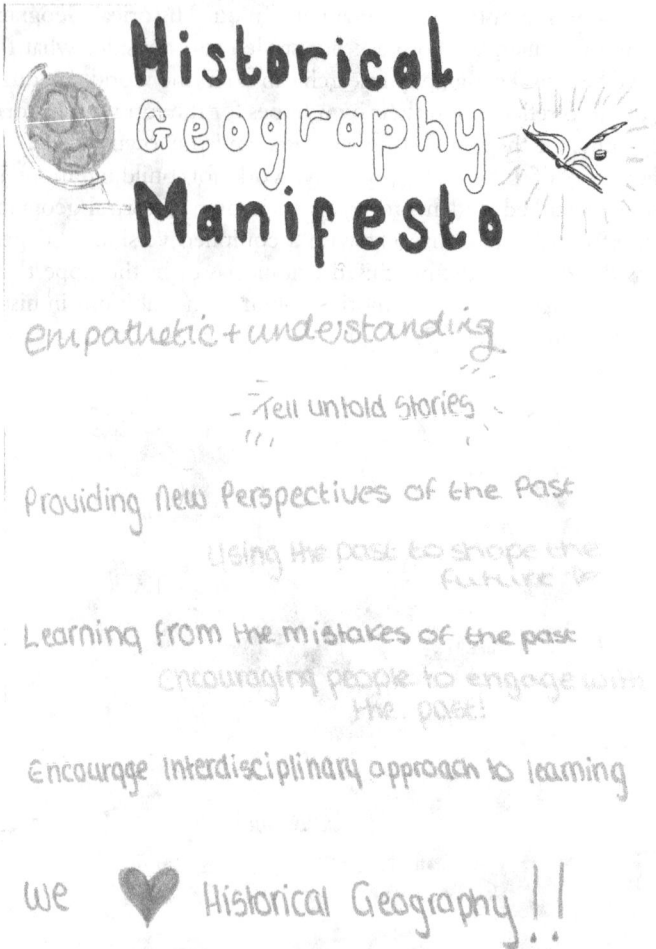

Historical Geography Manifesto

empathetic + understanding

- Tell untold stories

Providing new Perspectives of the Past

Using the past to shape the future

Learning from the mistakes of the past

Encouraging people to engage with the past!

Encourage interdisciplinary approach to learning

we ♥ Historical Geography !!

Amy, Ella, Diego, Nina and Alexander

Figure 7.3 Example manifesto 3 from Historical Geographies Honours Course 2024, University of Glasgow.

Source: author's own.

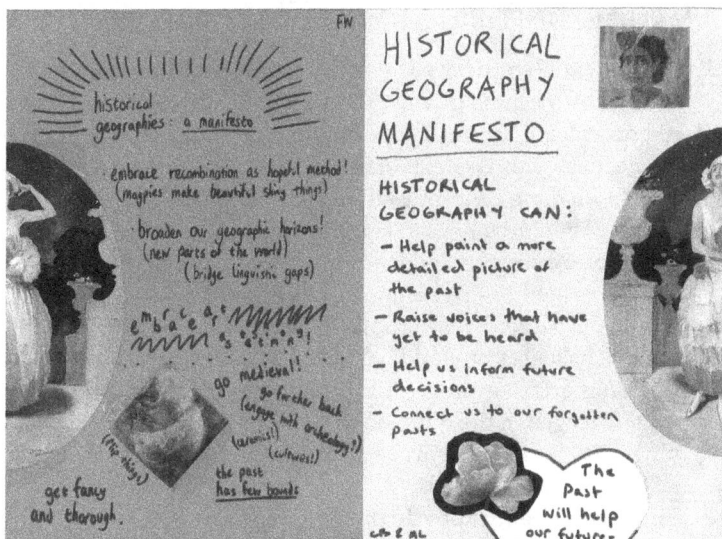

Figure 7.4 Example manifesto 4 from Historical Geographies Honours Course 2024, University of Glasgow.

Source: author's own.

Student work on our modules reflects these possibilities and below we give some indication of their project titles to indicate the diversity and vibrancy of historical geography:

BOX 7.2 Example work from historical geography modules

- Voices of escaped slaves – historical geographies of slavery
- UK miners' strike centenary – historical geographies of solidarity
- Revisiting Hillsborough – a football tragedy and emerging solidarity
- British women in colonial India – revisiting oral histories
- Conscientious objection and anti-war activism during the First World War
- Pirates in the eighteenth century – historical geographies of maritime violence
- Remembering Scottish witches – feminist historical geographies
- Ice cream wars and local histories – geographical biographies and place-writing

A MANIFESTO FOR HISTORICAL GEOGRAPHIES

1. **Historical Geography is committed to shaping *usable pasts***
   Whilst the meaning of what is 'usable' is likely to draw different responses from different perspectives, our work is committed to connecting with contemporary matters, perhaps societal injustices or ongoing conceptual thinking. The purpose of a return to the past should be considered when shaping a research agenda. Whether uncovering hidden histories or revisiting marginalised voices, or perhaps returning to more familiar pasts, our work should have a sense of purpose. This may be linked to contemporary challenges or could be fuelled by a devotion to a particular community or archive, but these commitments should be acknowledged in the question of why conduct historical geography. This question is never easy to answer but is one we should all continue to consider.

2. **Historical Geography is *theoretically driven***
   As discussed in Chapter 4, one of the distinctive features of historical geography is the emphasis upon theory in shaping our practice and our writing. We consider this to be absolutely central to the future of historical geography. By stressing the vital nature of theory we begin to show the wider relevance of a past. We also begin to acknowledge how we approach particular histories. We consider both elements as integral to the future of historical geography work.

3. **Historical Geography is *collaborative***
   Throughout both of our research careers we have drawn upon countless others in shaping our research and teaching of historical geography. We recognise that collaboration means different things to different people, but we are all reliant upon others in revisiting the past. It remains possible that you can plough your own path and be deeply connected to an individual project, but even this pursuit requires elements of collaboration. Recognising those that assist in our research shapes new opportunities for future partnerships which can lead to new research directions and possibilities. It also pushes us to acknowledge the resources required to research the past (see below).

4. **Historical Geography is dedicated to** *protecting pasts*

   Such collaborations include working with archives and people and/or organisations that preserve the past (libraries, museums, communities, etc.) in a context where archives are potentially at threat or may never have been established. As researchers we should recognise the resource required to preserve and maintain access to past lives and events, and value the labour and expertise that exists beyond academia to co-create our stories about the past.

5. **Historical Geography is committed to** *storying multiple pasts*

   A large part of this book has made reference to the idea of writing stories. Stories mean different things to different people but our task, as historical geographers, is to illuminate the past through insights and evidence which lead to the possibilities of storying the past. How we write about the past matters, and our approach will likely depend upon our own positionalities and audience. We have encouraged best practice as well as creativity. The type of stories we tell matters too and the book has encouraged a more pluralistic sense of the past in order to include marginalised perspectives and alternative histories.

6. **Historical Geography is** *committed to historical accuracy*

   We have continually stressed the potential of telling stories throughout this book. Our intention has been to encourage creativity in representing the past, but we do so with an important caveat. Creativity should not be at the expense of methodological rigor or historical accuracy. We should work with the archive to tell stories in a manner that is supported empirically. Historical work is committed to (re-)telling detailed accounts of the past. This makes archival work particularly crucial and places emphasis upon the accuracy of note keeping and how we interpret the archival document.

7. **Historical Geography must contemplate the** *ethical dimensions of revisiting pasts*

   In different places across this book, we have indicated how engaging with the past might be challenging and uncomfortable. Whether working through something personal and intimate, or finding something in the archive that might move or trouble you, historical geography has a responsibility to those pasts it looks to uncover. It is our job to tread carefully, to reflect on the potential impacts of using, or misusing, materials and to consider the wider impacts of our work. Whilst archival research might not necessarily require rigorous institutional ethical review, researchers retain responsibility for the pasts they tell. This is equally true for oral histories whereby our asking of people to recall past events and experiences should be conducted sensitively and carefully so not to cause harm to our participants.

8. **Historical Geography is** *exciting, vibrant and inspiring*
   Our final manifesto commitment is to recognise the wide-reaching potential of historical geography. As previously noted, we consider ourselves historical geographers in-the-making, learning through collaborations and ongoing research. In writing this book, we have (re-)discovered the vibrancy of work associated with geographical approaches to the past. The possibilities for further research are perhaps what excites us most, and our sense that there is a historical geography project for everyone. The exciting and uplifting nature of uncovering an archival item, or working with an individual in retracing their past, is something to be celebrated as we create our own journeys through historical geographies.

BOX 7.3 Exercise – Produce your own historical geography manifesto

Consider what your own manifesto for historical geography might include by asking yourself the question: what do I feel historical geography does in the world? What do I think are its key strengths? What are my hopes for the future of historical geography research?

List bullet points identifying some key principles for the sub-discipline and how you consider it should develop moving forward.

Are there any areas that require further research? Are there any forms of collaboration that should be further stressed? What formats should historical take in terms of outputs?

Our manifesto above is general and targeted at a wide-ranging historical geography grouping. Your manifesto might be more specific and bespoke to your own topics and particular interest in the past.

REFERENCES

Crawford, L. (2024) 'Emancipatory archival methods: Exploring the historical geographies of disability', *Area*, 56(1), p. e12844.

DeLyser, D. (2014) 'Towards a participatory historical geography: Archival interventions, volunteer service, and public outreach in research on early women pilots', *Journal of Historical Geography*, 46, pp. 93–98.

Hitchcock, D. (2013) 'Why history from below matters more than ever', the many-headed monster. Available online: https://manyheadedmonster.com/2013/07/22/david-hitchcock-why-history-from-below-matters-more-than-ever/. Last accessed: 11/4/2025.

McInerney, K. (2025) 'Reclaiming space: Enacting citizenship through embodied protest during the British Suffragette Movement', *Gender, Place & Culture*, 32(2), pp. 133–154.

Moore, F. (2018) 'Historical geography, feminist research and the gender politics of the present', *Geography Compass*, 12(9), p. e12398.

Morin, K. and Moran, D. (2015) *Historical geographies of prisons: Unlocking the usable carceral past*. London: Routledge.

INDEX

Note: page numbers in *italics* refer to figures and **bold** refer to tables.

For Product Safety Concerns and Information please contact our EU
representative GPSR@taylorandfrancis.com
Taylor & Francis Verlag GmbH, Kaufingerstraße 24, 80331 München, Germany